Anglican
and their Canons:

1549, Interim Rite and Roman

Mark Dalby

Archdeacon of Rochdale
Diocese of Manchester in the Church of England

GROVE BOOKS LIMITED
RIDLEY HALL RD CAMBRIDGE CB3 9HU

Contents

The Cover Illustration is a frontispiece from *The Anglican Missal*, published by The Society of SS. Peter and Paul in 1921, to which reference is made on pages 23-24 below.

First Impression September 1998
ISSN 0951-2667
ISBN 1 85174 384 7

1.
The Nineteenth Century

The 1549 prayer book retained much of the traditional shape of the mass. This shape was lost in the 1552 book, not least in its separation of the prayer of oblation from the prayer of consecration and its repositioning of it after the reception of communion. The new rite never commended itself to the more catholic-minded, and it was the practice of Bishop Overall of Norwich (1560-1619), as observed by his chaplain John Cosin, always

'to use this oblation in its right place, when he had consecrated the Sacrament to make an offering of it (as being the true public sacrifice of the Church) unto God ... that by the merits of Christ's death, which was now commemorated, all the Church of God might receive mercy, etc, as in this prayer; and when that was done he did communicate the people, and so end with the thanksgiving following hereafter'[1].

Cosin himself approved this order, and William Laud in the 1637 Scottish Liturgy[2] restored not only the 1549 order but also most of the 1549 content. The 1637 canon was very much what the Laudian school would have liked in the later English revision, and it was the model for the canon in the *Durham Book*. But 'it is clear that it was not a practicable proposition in the year 1661'. Accordingly 'My Lords the Bishops at Ely House ordered all in the old method', and 1662 was much the same as 1552[3].

In the eighteenth century men like John Sharp, archbishop of York, the liturgist Charles Wheatly and Thomas Wilson, bishop of Sodor and Man, all expressed their preference for the 1549 canon.[4] Overall's practice was revived in a number of Scottish congregations which otherwise adhered to 1662[5], while the 1764 Scottish canon and the 1790 American canon were based on 1637, though with the epiclesis in an eastern position after the institution narrative. But Englishmen were less fortunate, and John Johnson of Cranbrook (1662-1725) concluded

'Such priests and pious discerning laymen, as are convinced of the truth and necessity of the primitive Sacrifice, and do not think that the public provision for it is sufficient, have no proper remedy left, but to labour with prayers to God, and with persuasions and arguments to men, for the perfect restitution of the sacrificial oblatory part of the Christian Liturgy; and in the meantime, to supply such defects as well as they can by their own private silent devotions.'[6]

---

1   J Cosin, 'Notes and Collections on the Book of Common Prayer', 1st Series, *Works* (Oxford, 1855), V: pp 114f.
2   Cf 'History of the Troubles and Trials', *Works* (Oxford, 1853), III:344.
3   G J Cuming, 'The Making of the Prayer Book of 1662' in *The English Prayer Book 1549-1662*, (1963), p.110, and ed G J Cuming, *The Durham Book* (Durham, 1961), pp 164-80.
4   T Sharp, *The Life of John Sharp* (1825), 1:355; C Wheatly, *Rational Illustration* 6.22.3, (ed 1848) p 299; T Wilson, *Sacra Privata*, ed Oxford and London, 1853, p 104. For similar opinions, cf W J Sparrow Simpson, *The Prayer of Consecration*, (1917), and W J Grisbrooke, *Anglican Liturgies of the Seventeenth and Eighteenth Centuries*, (1958).
5   Cf W J Grisbrooke, *op.cit.* ch.8 *passim*.
6   'The Unbloody Sacrifice', *Works*, (Oxford, 1847), 1:17.

From 1662 to 1860 there were many manuals for lay people who wished to offer 'their own private silent devotions' at the eucharist[1], and Bishop Wilson's *Sacra Privata* shows that such devotions were not confined to lay people.[2] How far these manuals were used at the altar it is impossible to estimate, but in the generation after the Oxford Movement such use became more common, and in 1866, in a book entitled *Ritual Inaccuracies*, H D Gressell, the honorary sub-sacristan of the Society of the Blessed Sacrament, complained that 'It is a general habit with many priests to carry to the altar a book for private devotion.'[7] Such books now became more common, but sometimes what began as a supplementary book developed into an alternative book, and supplementary books were soon rendered unnecessary by a succession of unofficial altar-books which offered the celebrant not only the statutory rite of the Prayer Book but also all the 'private devotion' he could possibly require and much more besides.

The first book deliberately designed as a supplement at the altar was *The Priest to the Altar, or Aids to the Devout Celebration of Holy Communion, Chiefly after the Ancient English Use of Sarum*. The first edition, octavo, was privately printed in 1861 and sold only to subscribers. Although clearly intended for use at the altar, as well as before and after the service, it could be used at the altar only alongside—or bound up with—the ordinary Prayer book as it did not contain the collects or lections. These latter however were included in a second edition published by Rivingtons in 1869. A third edition, quarto, was published by Rivingtons in 1879, a fourth by Longmans in 1898, and a fifth by the Oxford University Press and Longmans in 1904. Each edition except the fifth was an enlargement of its predecessor.

The first three editions were published anonymously, and at one time the work was attributed to H P Liddon[4], who from 1870 was a canon of St Paul's. Liddon may well have been its inspiration[5]—he was certainly consulted, as were various other Oxford men—but the actual compiler was Peter Goldsmith Medd, a young fellow of University College. Medd's approach to liturgy was that of a devout user rather than of a scholar in the narrow sense. He had a high regard for the Prayer Book, 'Those who know most about it and use it most, these value and love it most'[6], and, apart from its additional prayers and lections, *The Priest to the Altar* was very much a traditional communicants' manual adapted for the use of the celebrant. Its rubrics were only slightly fuller than those of the prayer book, and its doctrinal and liturgical standpoint was 'strictly that of the Reformed Catholic or Anglican Church'.[7] While Sarum was the main

1 Cf J Wickham Legg, *English Church Life from the Restoration to the Tractarian Movement*, (1914) pp 57-65, 338-50.
2 *Ed.cit*, p 104-06.
3 *Ritual Inaccuracies*, p.21.
4 W McGarvey and C P A Burnett, *The Ceremonies of the Mass*, (New York, 1905), p iii.
5 Cf E Milner-White, 'Modern Prayers and their Writers' in *Liturgy and Worship*, ed W K L Clarke and C Harris (SPCK, 1932), p 756.
6 *On the Liturgy of the Church of England*, (1898), p 28.
7 Preface to fourth edition, p vi

source of the supplementary material, Medd also drew from early sacramentaries and eastern liturgies as well from other English uses and from forms authorized by the Convocations or other parts of the Anglican Communion.

The first edition contained three parts. Part one consisted of preparatory material from such writers as Thomas a Kempis and Bishop Ken. Part two contained the 1662 service 'with some directions and private devotions for the celebrant' and offices of preparation and thanksgiving. Part three included 'Secrets, Postcommunions, Prayers for the People, and Benedictions, throughout the year' (the last two to be said during the office of thanksgiving), prayers 'for various objects and occasions', devotions and hymns. The second edition began with the prayer-book calendar interleaved, and included the collects and lections along with the secrets etc. The third edition added more collects and lections for special occasions, and also printed in full the 1549, Scottish and American rites. The fourth edition relegated the 1549 rite to an appendix where it appeared in small type along with the Latin text of the Sarum rite, but it added in the main text forms for the commemoration of the departed.

In the Prayer Book communion service the rubrics were printed in red, additional rubrics and private devotions were carefully bracketed, and the main features of the rite were printed in larger type. Nothing was added for public recitation except, in the later editions, the responses before and after the gospel, but there were many significant silent interpolations. In the ante-communion these consisted of *Aufer a nobis* and Psalm 43, provision for occasional collects after the collect for purity (in the fourth edition, after the collect for the Queen), benedictions before the gospel, and 1 Chron 29.10 from the Scottish liturgy at the placing of the alms on the holy table. In the prayer for the church militant, three marginal rubrics—'*Oblation of the Elements*', '*Here let him remember the living*', and '*Here let him remember the departed*'—equated the prayer, as its 1549 position had suggested, with the twofold *Memento* of the Gelasian canon. In the first edition, after the prayer of humble access came the secret and *In spiritu humilitatis*, which corresponded with the petition of *Te igitur* for the acceptance of the gifts, and after the ordering of the bread and wine came an epiclesis. In later editions however *In spiritu humilitatis* and the secret—either from the coronation service or of the day—were brought forward to their traditional place at the conclusion of the offertory, and immediately before the prayer of consecration brief extracts from the Gelasian canon were printed as an alternative to the epiclesis.

The canon was to prove a major problem in almost all the unofficial missals, and Medd's treatment of it varied from edition to edition. In the first edition, it was suggested that the priest might say 'secretly the Prayer of Oblation' either from the Sarum Use (*Unde et Memores* and *Supra quae propitio*) or according to the English Office of 1549 and the present Scottish and American Uses ('Wherefore O Lord . . . procured unto us by the same'). The *Agnus Dei* came next, then the pre-communion prayers and a prayer after reception. The 1662 prayer of oblation, in its 1662 position after the communion, was printed in large type, in contrast to the small type employed for the prayer of thanksgiving, and was annotated 'The Oblation' and 'The Oblation of Ourselves'. After the blessing were added the ablution prayers, provisions for a post-communion, *Placeat tibi*, and *'returning from the Altar'* the last gospel.

The great weakness of this scheme lay in its confused treatment of the oblation. Medd regarded the oblation as an essential feature of the rite and saw the 1549 office where the prayer was said publicly immediately after the consecration as 'the true model of a genuine English liturgy'[1]; the 1552 transference of it to a position after the communion (where it was only an optional alternative to the prayer of thanksgiving) was 'needless, wanton and unhappy'.[2] He was well aware of Bishop Overall's seventeenth-century remedy, but he was unable to follow this himself for a public recitation of the oblation here violated his further principle that under present conditions the public parts of the service and their positions should be strictly in accordance with 1662. Nor was he able to accept the modified form of Overall's position, suggested (though not preferred) by John Purchas in 1858, of reciting the 1662 prayer *'secreto* after the consecration'[3], for this violated a third principle that there must always be a public oblation.

Medd's initial solution of recommending extracts from the Sarum or 1549 oblations privately after the consecration and the 1662 oblation publicly after the communion was a bold attempt to satisfy all his principles, but it involved a duplication which created more problems than it solved. In the second edition the prayer of thanksgiving was printed in large type as well as the prayer of oblation—an indication that some celebrants might omit the 1662 oblation if they preferred a private oblation, in what they deemed the right place, to a public one in the wrong place. But there was now developing a demand for the occasional use of the 1549 rite as a permissive alternative, and in the third edition, as already noted, this was inserted *in toto* in large type immediately after 1662—along with the Scottish and American rites, also in large type— presumably in the hope of its eventual authorization. By the time of the fourth edition, however, Medd was arguing 'that, after three centuries' experience, something even better might now be framed which should preserve the main features, in order and arrangement, of the Service to which we have grown accustomed.'[4] He now relegated 1549 to an appendix and deleted the extracts from the 1549 canon which had previously appeared after the prayer of consecration. Henceforth the traditional oblation was made only in its traditional place and with its traditional words, *Unde et memores* and (in this edition) *Supplices te rogamus*. The 1662 prayer of oblation remained in large type in its 1662 position, but duplication was minimized in that the annotation 'The Oblation' was removed and the prayer remained, no doubt as Cranmer had intended it, simply as 'The Oblation of Ourselves'.

1   Introduction to *The First Book of Common Prayer of Edward VI*, (ed H B Walton, 1869), p xx, f.
2   *On the Liturgy of the Church of England*, 1898, p 23.
3   *Directorium Anglicanum*, 1st edn, p 58.
4   *On the Liturgy of the Church of England*, 1898, p 24.

The second book was published in 1867 by Frederick George Lee, who has been variously described as 'an accomplished historian and antiquary' and, more accurately perhaps, as 'a considerable, but inexact, liturgical scholar'.[1] Lee had collaborated with Purchas in the first edition of the *Directorium Anglicanum,* 'a Manual of Directions for the Right Celebration of the Holy Communion . . . According to Ancient Uses of the Church of England' which appeared under Purchas' name in 1858 and which sought to accommodate the rubrics of the Prayer Book to the ceremonial of Sarum. But the second edition in 1865 had appeared under Lee's name, as had the third edition in 1866. Although all editions printed the second part of the Gelasian canon, *Unde et Memores,* in a way that could be used at the altar, they were clearly intended primarily for the study or the sacristy.

In 1867, however, the year when he became vicar of All Saints Lambeth, Lee edited three books specifically designed 'for the use of the priest, the gospeller and the epistoler in the ministry of the altar'. In his introduction, he explained that 'the need of suitable books for use in the service of the Altar, which so many have experienced during the present Revival, has led to this publication' and that 'when the Holy Eucharist is being restored to its proper place amongst the services of the sanctuary, many have regretted that books, modelled after the ancient form, were not to be procured.' He lamented that the original small folio volumes had long since been replaced by less convenient large quartos, and his own volumes were large folios with wide margins, handsomely produced by Thomas Bosworth and the Chiswick Press. They followed where possible 'the form, plan, and arrangements of the ancient Service Books', Sarum as well as post-reformation; and *The Altar Service Book,* i.e. 'the Service Book for the Priest Celebrant' also included, like other contemporary altar books, Confirmation, Marriage and the Ordinal. Lee claimed that this book contained all that could be required by the priest 'either for Low or High Celebration', but this was not invariably true for the book appeared in two forms, one with plainsong tones for the Creed, the Comfortable Words, the Sursum Corda, the Preface and Sanctus, the Our Father, Gloria and Blessing, but the other without music at any point. Music apart, however, the two forms were identical, and Lee was careful to claim authority whenever he deviated from the customary presentation of the rite. Thus in the order for Holy Communion,

'Following Catholic precedent—a precedent which obtained as well in the Plaintain editions of the *Missale Romanum* as in the various editions of the pre-Reformation English Missals, and is still retained in the Oriental Churches—a picture of the Crucifixion has been placed opposite the Canon.'

The canon was broken up into paragraphs, the words of consecration printed in capital letters (as was the *incarnatus* in the creed), the manual directions were

1 Cf S Morison, *English Prayer Books,* (Cambridge, 1949), 3rd edn, p 152; H R T Brandreth, *Dr Lee of Lambeth,* 1951, p 12.

incorporated in the main text and the sign of the cross was inserted at various points (as also in the Absolution and the Blessing) while a collect, epistle and gospel were provided for use at funerals.

Lee's *Altar Service Book* was infinitely more modest in content than *The Priest to the Altar*, and it contained none of the advanced ritual recommended in the *Directorium Anglicanum*. He was bold enough to dedicate all three of his volumes to Archbishop Longley and he duly presented him with copies, but the latter was not impressed,

'When you did me the favour of leaving at Lambeth Palace large paper copies of the Reprints of the Communion Service, and of the Epistles and Gospels, I accepted them under the full impression that they were merely a reprint of them from our Prayer Book. Finding, however, that this is not the case and that certain liberties have been taken with the Prayer Book, of which I do not approve, I feel myself compelled to decline keeping them. I will take an early opportunity of sending them back to you.'[1]

But Lee does not seem to have been deterred. Many years later he presented the three altar books to St Paul's Cathedral where they were still in use in the 1950s, and, although these particular books were not reprinted, in 1874 he published the *Manuale Clericorum*, a shortened and simplified version of the *Directorium*, and in 1878 he published a fourth edition of the *Directorium* itself.

Neither of the books considered so far provided everything which their diverse users required. Many—possibly most—surviving copies of *The Priest to the Altar* have handwritten, or later typed, additions and insertions at various points, while a copy of *The Altar Service Book* has survived in which were inserted—hand-painted in beautiful script with illuminated initials—the Roman form of the preparation, the Gelasian canon and the last gospel along with collects and lections for 13 additional feasts.[2] Individual insertions of one kind or another, and occasional deletions, made according to the needs and preferences of particular priests, were to become almost the norm in unofficial missals, and they persist to this day. But both books, or at least their editors, had had as their main inspiration the pre-reformation Sarum rite or, to a lesser extent, the first Prayer Book of 1549. Knowledge of the Sarum rite had been disseminated by a number of scholarly publications[3], and it was natural that those who stressed the continuity between the contemporary church and the pre-reformation church should look to Sarum. But the Sarum rite had not been used for more than three hundred years, and it was equally natural that those who stressed the catholic nature of the contemporary church should look to the present rites of the rest of the Western Catholic Church, i.e. to Rome. In 1868-69 the Society of the Holy Cross (SSC)

1   Brandreth, *op. cit.* p 164.
2   This copy is now at St Peter, London Dock, though its condition suggests it was hardly ever used. I am grateful to the present parish priest, Fr Trevor Jones, for information about the books at St Peter's.
3   Eg W Maskell, *The Ancient Liturgy according to the Uses of Sarum, Bangor, York and Hereford*, 2nd edn 1846; A H Pearson, *The Sarum Missal, done into English*, 1868.

expressed a corporate preference from the Roman rite[1], and if the treatment of the canon was to provide one source of division among Anglican catholics, the merits of ancient Sarum or 'the English use' against modern Rome or 'the Western rite' was now to provide another.[2]

Some who preferred the Roman use opted simply for *Missale Romanum* in Latin and ignored Anglican usage altogether[3], but these were a minority and the next altar-book, *The Ritual of the Altar*, published by Longmans in 1870 in a small octavo, was designed for those who felt some degree of obligation to the Prayer Book but who wished to enrich it by contemporary Roman provision rather than that of ancient Sarum. Like the first edition of *The Priest to the Altar* it lacked the Prayer Book propers, but the preface explicitly stated that it was to be 'used by the Priest at the time of Divine Service' as well as for reference, and that it would conveniently 'bind up with the "Sealed Copy" of the Prayer Book, or its edition of the Collects, Epistles, and Gospels, as published by Mr Masters'.[4] A second edition, much enlarged and including the propers, was issued in quarto in 1878 and was finely printed with rubrics in red by the Chiswick Press; by the end of 1882 all copies had been sold, but the publishers were left with a loss of £56.15.7½d.[5]

The compiler of *The Ritual of the Altar*, Orby Shipley, was a prolific author, editor and translator, and he was also a member of the SSC. In 1866, in the first of three symposia which he edited on questions of the day, each entitled *The Church and the World*, he published an essay of his own on 'The Liturgies of 1549 and 1662, Contrasted and Compared'. Like Medd he regarded 1549 as 'the standard of ritual of the modern English church'.[6] The structural difference of the later rite was 'exceedingly great', and the revision of the canon, which had been 'at once decapitated and curtailed', had 'run to the freest extent of riot'.[7] He also issued in 1866 a small booklet, *The Liturgies of 1549 and 1662*, which contained the bulk of the two offices printed on parallel pages. Here he gave clear warning that

'Although under existing circumstances any alteration in the Prayer Book is deprecated by the Church party, yet, if a revision of our Offices be determined upon by the only authority we can admit, a large and powerful body composed of laymen and clergymen, will exert its influence to secure a restoration of our present Book of Common Prayer in conformity with the First Book of King Edward VI.'[8]

1 Cf W Walsh, *The Secret History of the Oxford Movement* (6th edn 1899), p 77.
2 For a later and dispassionate summary of the issues, cf S Gaselee, 'The Aesthetic Side of the Oxford Movement' in N P Williams and C Harris (ed), *Northern Catholicism*, (1933), pp 429-32.
3 P F Anson, *The Call of the Cloister*, (4th edn 1964), p 402, states that the Sisters of the Poor, founded in 1865, always used *Missale Romanum* in their chapels at Shoreditch and Edgware
4 p xiii.
5 Information kindly supplied by the archives and manuscripts department of the University of Reading which holds the Longman archives.
6 p 504
7 p 513f.
8 p xvi,ff

The partiality expressed here for 1549 is a poor preparation for *The Ritual of the Altar*, for its inspiration was not 1549 but, as we have noted, *Missale Romanum*. 1662, 'that form of word and act to which we are by our position pledged'[1], was printed verbatim, with rubrics and prayers in full, but to it were added 'all the prayers and every direction from the Ordinary and Canon of the Mass by which the Liturgy of the English Church may be supplemented'.[2] This, Shipley argued, was a natural and logical course,

'If it were permissible for the compilers of the English Use in the sixteenth century to adapt materials from the Roman Missal for public recitation, it cannot be disloyal to take advantage of the same materials for the private edification of members of the same Church in the nineteenth century—always supposing, which is emphatically asserted, that one principle underlies both.'[3]

The Prayer Book had been compiled 'almost on the principle of giving the minimum of direction'. *The Ritual of The Altar* was compiled 'almost on the principle of giving the maximum'.[4]

The first edition began with a preface which was followed by the preparation and thanksgiving and then the ordinary and canon. There followed the propers of the season and of the saints—collects and lections for days for which the Prayer Book made no provision: ember days, vigils, additional feasts of the Blessed Virgin Mary etc—the common of saints, various propers for such occasions as the dedication of a church, votive masses, masses of the dead and memorials of the departed. It concluded with an appendix containing general rubrics adapted for Anglican use from *Ritus Servandus*.

The ordinary and canon included rubrical directions, private prayers and ritual music for the priest, and also directions for his assistants. Additional rubrics were enclosed in square brackets, and the private prayers were printed in small type and in parallel columns of Latin and English, the Latin being recommended. The asperges, preparation, gospel ceremonies, offertory, canon and last gospel were all interpolated in strict accordance with the Roman rite. The only occasions when the Roman provisions were not printed was when they could only be rendered audibly or when they directly contradicted or duplicated the provisions of the Prayer Book. This meant that there were no additional propers except introits and graduals, no kyries and no salutations, that the Our Father and gloria were printed after the communion, and that the ablutions were placed at the end of the rite. But there was still confusion with regard to the prayer of oblation. Overall's practice was dismissed as a 'partial and imperfect restoration of the ancient form'[5], but despite the oblation in the Gelasian canon the 1662 oblation was still to be recited after the communion. It

1   p xx.
2   p xiii
3   p xvii.
4   p xli,f.
5   p xix note 2.

was printed in large type and accompanied by three signations, while the prayer of thanksgiving was printed only in small type and with the bracketed note, 'which may be said at a Communion for the Sick' when presumably communion was given from the reserved sacrament. In the second edition, however, this note was omitted and the two prayers were printed in similar type—a further indication that the 1662 oblation in its 1662 position was falling into disfavour.

This second edition was much more ambitious, both in format and content. A new preface proclaimed that *'The Ritual of the Altar* aspires to be, though it is not called, a Missal for daily use in the English Church', and a general rearrangement placed its contents 'in harmony, so far as is possible, with those of existing Missals'. The Prayer-Book kalendar was printed at the beginning, with four additional holy-days and all feasts carefully classified; the Prayer Book collects and lections were included along with the full proper for all feasts: introit, gradual, offertory, secret, communion and postcommunion; and all prayers and lessons were 'punctuated for use of ecclesiastical chant'. Further additions included Benediction of the Most Holy Sacrament, divers benedictions, and the order of ceremonies for Candlemas, Lent and Easter.

To save space a number of omissions were made. These included the Latin originals of the private prayers and even of the canon, the non-ceremonial rubrics from the beginning and end of 1662, all the 1662 offertory sentences except the first and the last, and also the longer exhortations. This meant of course that the Prayer Book rite was no longer printed *verbatim*, and, while space may indeed have been one reason for the omissions, there were other unmistakeable indications that loyalty to the Prayer Book was weakening. Prayer Book rubrics were no longer distinguished from Roman ones, the ninefold kyrie was printed after the ten commandments, salutations were inserted, Roman formulae for introducing the lessons were printed alongside the Prayer Book ones, twelve additional prefaces were included from the Roman rite, the Our Father was printed after the canon as well as after the communion, and the ablutions were brought forward to the Roman position.

But despite its weakened loyalty to the Prayer Book, *The Ritual of the Altar* was essentially a disciplined book which could proudly describe itself as 'a missal . . . unauthorised indeed, but not without authority'. This authority, when not that of the Prayer Book, was that of *Missale Romanum*, and only on three occasions did Shipley allow his private judgment to prevail: the addition of the Dominical summary of the law from the Scottish rite as an alternative to the ten commandments or kyries; the addition from Sarum, in the absence of any Roman parallel, of the post-reception prayer, *Ave in eternum*; and the choice of Sarum introits etc to accompany the Prayer Book collects and lections on the ground that, Sarum being the main source of these lections, the accompanying Sarum propers were more harmonious therewith than their modern Roman equivalents.

In 1876 another Sarum book, *Notes on Ceremonial*, was published by Pickering in a small octavo, having been compiled—like its companion volumes, *Ceremonial for Servers* (1876; later *Altar Servers' Ceremonial*, 9th edn still in print 1928), *Priests'*

Ceremonial (1888; 4th edn, 1928) and *A Chart of Ceremonial* (1904)—by a Devonshire rector, Herbert George Morse. As its title indicated, *Notes on Ceremonial* was primarily a ceremonial guide, and 'The order for the celebration of the Holy Eucharist with the *Secreta* from the Sarum Missal', with which the first edition concluded, was little more than an appendix. But in the second (1882), third (1888) and fourth (1895) editions—printed in royal octavo at the Chiswick Press—this order was placed 'at the beginning instead of at the end of the book, for the convenience of those who may wish to bind it up with an ordinary altar-book without including the chapters containing ceremonial directions'. In the third and fourth editions rubrics were in red, but the contents of the order varied little from one edition to another, and broadly speaking it integrated the 1662 communion service with that of Sarum in much the same moderate way that the first edition of *The Ritual of the Altar* integrated it with that of Rome.

Prayers before celebrating and the form for the blessing of water preceded the order, and the thanksgiving followed it. In the order itself some of the additional rubrics were bracketed, but not all; large and small types were employed in the second and subsequent editions, but their use denoted the importance of the prayers, not their source. The preparation, the blessing of water, the gospel ceremonies, the offertory prayers, the canon and the prayers which followed it were all interpolated in their Sarum form, and rubrical provision was made for introits and graduals. Salutations, optional from the second edition onwards, were inserted before the collect, gospel, and (later) sursum corda, and the benedictus was added 'in a low voice' after the sanctus. In the first edition, the Lord's Prayer appeared only after the communion, but in subsequent editions it was printed after the canon as well. The ablutions were taken after the blessing, and the last gospel said 'in returning' from the altar. In the second edition ritual music was added, and in the third and fourth editions an epistle and gospel were added for use 'at funerals, and on All Souls Day'.

The Gelasian canon was printed in large type, the earlier sections appearing before the prayer of humble access. In the first two editions *Quam oblationem* was omitted on the ground that it duplicated the first part of the 1662 prayer of consecration[1], but it was included in later editions though only in small type. In the second and later editions *Supra quae propitios*, a clause in *Supplices te rogamus*, and *Per quem haec omnia* were also in small or broken type; Morse regarded them as unsuitable for use after consecration since they 'are survivals from a more ancient arrangement of the canon, in which these passages occurred before the consecration.'[2]

From the time of its second edition *Notes on Ceremonial* had looked as if it might well expand into a complete missal, but in the fifth (1911) and sixth (1921) editions its original ceremonial concern was reasserted and the communion service was omitted altogether. The reader was reminded that the

---

1   1st edn, p 84.
2   2nd edn, p 134.

communion service could still be found 'printed in clear type for use at the altar, together with private prayers for the Celebrant' in *Priests' Ceremonial*. But this latter, a small octavo printed throughout in black, dealt only with plain celebrations; it lacked the ritual music, and in general was a poor substitute.

The next missal was *Divine Service*, an octavo book of similar size to the later *English Missal for the Laity*. It was described as 'a complete Office Book and Manual of Devotions for the Laity, assisting and communicating at the Holy Sacrifice, and a great help and guide to the Clergy in celebrating the Divine Mysteries' and, although it was clearly designed primarily for the laity, memories of copies where the canon was 'tabbed' indicate that some clergy did indeed use it at the altar.[1] It was first published in 1878 by G J Palmer, and its last (3rd) edition was published in 1909 by W Walker. The anonymous editor, who may have been Henry Daniel Nihill, vicar of St Michael Shoreditch and again a member (and later master) of the SSC, drew from Sarum, Rome and Paris as well as from other sources, but although he made much use of Sarum his basic inspiration was probably Roman. The book began with preparations and thanksgivings and continued with 'the divine service', the proper of the season and of saints, the common of saints, masses of commemoration etc and divers collects. Strangely 'the divine service' appeared in three forms—'assisting at the sacrifice, for worship and spiritual communion; 'assisting at the holy sacrifice, for communion' and 'offering the holy sacrifice for the rest of the departed'. The canon was that of 1662 preceded and followed by the Gelasian canon, and there was no suggestion of the use of the prayer of oblation before the communion.

In 1886 Rivingtons published *The Altar Book*, an edition of 1662 similar to, though smaller than, Lee's book and very much in the style of *The Priest to the Altar* without the latter's supplementary material, and this was reprinted in 1892. This book was of only minor importance, but in 1894 Rivingtons published an *Altar Book containing the Order of Holy Communion According to the Use of the Church of England with Additions from the Sarum Missal*. This second *Altar Book*, a large quarto, was the first unofficial missal to include in its first edition all the prayer-book collects and lections and thus, unlike its predecessors, to be complete in itself from the very beginning. It was also the only comprehensive missal ever to be published on strictly Sarum lines, and, with a reprint in 1902, a second edition in 1914 and a third in 1930, it was the only nineteenth-century missal to remain in print till the 1960s. It was edited by an anonymous 'committee of priests', under the leadership of Salisbury James Murray Price who was vicar of St Ives in Huntingdonshire from 1894-99, and the principles on which it was compiled and the additions which it offered were much the same as those of its Roman counterpart, *The Ritual of the Altar*. It was rather more advanced than the first edition of that book but less advanced than the second

---

1 Letter to the writer from Fr F E P Langton, 1966; Langton thought, despite Anson (note 3 on p 11 *supra)*, that it was used for a while by the sisters at Shoreditch. Anson, *op. cit.* p 96 n.2, pointed out that there were many similarities between this book and *The Day Office of the Church*, 'the most popular diurnal among the more extreme Ritualists'.

edition. Its contents were much the same except that the preparation and thanksgiving, the general rubrics and the rite of Benediction were all omitted.

The kalendar was that of the Prayer Book, with the addition of Sarum ranks and octaves and of two extra feasts: Assumption of the B.V.M. and St Thomas of Canterbury. The proper of the season, however, added the full proper for all those days which had formerly been observed by Sarum, the most notable being Wednesdays and Fridays throughout the year and the weekdays of Lent, while an appendix in smaller type included ceremonies for Ash Wednesday, Holy Week and Candlemas, the lessons for Whitsun Eve and the order of the procession on Easter Day. 'The Ordinary and Canon of the Mass, together with the Order of Communion' was printed in red and black and accompanied by full rubrical directions, private prayers, ritual music and notes on singing the epistle and gospel (though the lessons themselves were not pointed). Its contents were very similar to those of the order in *Notes on Ceremonial*. The 1662 rite was printed *in toto*, though shorn of some of its rubrics, and the preparation, blessing of water, gospel ceremonies, offertory prayers and canon were all inserted in their Sarum form. There was no typographical distinction between Sarum and Prayer Book material, though many of the additions were bracketed. Almost invariably the Prayer Book took precedence, and with the exception of the ninefold kyrie in English as an alternative to the commandments and the recitation of the Lord's Prayer before the communion as well as after it, Sarum material was not inserted when it contradicted or duplicated that of the Prayer Book; on the same principle the ablutions were printed in their 1662 position after the blessing. There was no hesitation, however, in introducing Sarum material even for audible recitation when it merely supplemented the Prayer Book, and provision was made for all the propers and salutations, the introduction to the gospel, and the benedictus, though not, as in *The Ritual of the Altar*, for additional prefaces. The Gelasian canon was printed in full and accompanied by its traditional rubrical directions, the earlier sections, as in *Notes on Ceremonial*, being printed before the prayer of humble access.

But many 'English' catholics were unhappy with all this and felt that the provisions of these books, even when inspired by Sarum rather than modern Roman usage, were in varying degrees inconsistent with a proper loyalty to the Prayer Book. In 1897 the Alcuin Club was founded with the guiding principle of 'strict obedience to the Book of Common Prayer', and in one of its earliest tracts, *Liturgical Interpolations*, T A Lacey strongly condemned the practice of 'interpolating into the English rite portions of another rite essential ritual in their character and use'.[1] He agreed that the 1662 rite could be improved, not least by the adoption of Overall's canon[2], but such improvements were not essential for 'Where there is Consecration, there is the Sacrifice'[3]. He concluded,

---

1   Tract 3, 1898, p 10.
2   *Ibid* p 21.
3   *Ibid* p 13.

'If any priest will abandon his interpolations and celebrate Mass according to the English liturgy exactly as it stands, I am convinced (and I speak not without experience) that he will find there an unlooked for beauty and dignity, and will offer the Holy Sacrifice with more joy to himself, and with more acceptance on high, since to obey is better even than sacrifice itself.'[1]

But the Alcuin Club represented only one group. The 1890s also saw the first publication of 'particular' missals, and in 1898 W Knott printed 'for private circulation' a quarto book clearly intended for the altar and entitled *The Ordinary, Canon & Proper of Mass for the Dead together with The Absolutions and other Prayers for the Faithful Departed*. Here, the 1662 communion service was integrated with the Roman form in a now familiar way with the Gelasian canon surrounding the prayer of consecration, though the Lord's Prayer was printed only after the communion and no attempt was made to distinguish between the prayer of oblation and the prayer of thanksgiving. This volume was later published generally as *The Requiem Missal*, while another version is believed to have been edited by 'a committee of priests' on Sarum lines.

---

1   *Ibid* p 20.

2.
Before 1928

At the beginning of the twentieth century there were only two complete alternatives to the official BCP in print: *The Priest to the Altar*, now in its fourth edition of 1898, and the *Altar Book* of 1894, still in its first edition. Both embodied Sarum usage, and in both the Gelasian canon was printed around the prayer of consecration, though neither now provided for the use of the prayer of oblation immediately after the consecration. At this period the various interpolations were still regarded largely as private priestly devotions and, since the Roman Catholic mass was still said for the most part silently, this attitude was not wholly untenable. Thus at a typical anglo-catholic mass the priest would continue after the consecration with the silent Gelasian canon while the congregation sang an appropriate hymn of adoration. There were no significant audible additions to the official rite, but the eucharistic sacrifice was offered explicitly, if silently, by the priest, while the congregation adored the Lord now sacramentally present.[1]

But the dominance of Sarum was only apparent. In 1902 Knott published for the Roman party a small quarto edition of *Votive Masses for the Use of the Church of England*. This was a modest production, printed throughout in black and in small type, with simplified rubrics, no music, and obviously intended for use at low masses, but its version of the ordinary and canon was almost entirely Roman and the Prayer Book provisions were largely ignored.

The Prayer Book party, inspired perhaps by the Alcuin Club, was also active. It resisted to some extent the blandishments of Sarum and certainly those of Rome, but it still sought more elegant altar books than those of the privileged presses or Rivington's 1886/92 edition, and the next three books, all issued in 1903, sought to satisfy this need. *The Altar Service Book according to the Use of the Church of England* was published by the De La More press in large octavo and printed in fine style, with the canon in large type and in red and black; 100 copies were printed on Japanese vellum and 600 more on handmade paper. The compiler was Vernon Staley, then Provost of Inverness. A convinced advocate of the English use, he was also a prolific writer, being author of some fifty books, including *The Ceremonial of the English Church*, and editor of the important *Library of Liturgiology and Ecclesiology*.[2]

The basis of *The Altar Service Book* was *The Communion Service according to the Use of the Church of England*, a straightforward following of 1662. The two were

1 Cf E C R Lamburn, *The Liturgy Develops*, (1960), p 33, and for an excellent summary of the later period pp 40-59.
2 Cf Martin Dudley, 'Vernon Staley' in C Irvine (ed), *They Shaped our Worship*, (Alcuin/SPCK, 1998), pp 29-34.

issued at the same time, and the only difference was that in *The Altar Service Book* forty-five additional pages with separate roman pagination were inserted at two suitable points. The first insertion, after the kalendar, consisted of notes on the kalendar and the occurrence of festivals and also on the ornaments rubric, altar lights and liturgical colours. The second insertion, immediately before the communion service, consisted of brief Sarum devotions before celebrating, when vesting (*Veni creator*), on approaching the altar (Psalm 43 and *Aufer a nobis*) and after celebrating. Strictly speaking all this additional material pertained more to the sacristy than to the altar. What was needed at the altar was music, which *The Altar Service Book* did not provide. In 1904 however a special supplement, *Altar Music*, was issued by Francis Burgess on the basis of G H Palmer's 1888 edition; this included Roman music as well as Sarum.

The third book issued in 1903 was *The English Liturgy from the Book of Common Prayer with Additional Collects, Epistles and Gospels*. An extra quarto volume, published by Rivingtons and 'sumptuously' printed throughout in red and black, it was an immediate success and was reprinted in 1909, 1914, 1920, 1930 and 1950. The chief compiler was Percy Dearmer who, as vicar of St Mary's, Primrose Hill, was fast establishing the 'Anglican Use', a modified version of Sarum which he had set forth in *The Parson's Handbook* four years previously. His co-compilers were W H Frere, CR, later Bishop of Truro; S M Taylor, later Bishop of Kingston; G H Palmer who edited the music; and E S Talbot, Bishop of Rochester, who wrote the preface.[1]

The first part of the book consisted of the kalendar, the rubrics and canons bearing on the communion, the office itself with ritual music but—'in accordance with a real principle'—without 'the inclusion of any extraneous matter whatever'[2], and the collects, epistles and gospels, including those from the ordinal and accession service, all pointed for singing. Now that *The Ritual of the Altar* had gone out of print, *The English Liturgy* was—and was to remain—the only altar book with the readings pointed, but initially its most distinctive feature, marked by a difference in type, was an appendix which brought together 'material for use on special days or occasions, which has already the sanction of usage and authority' and 'a small amount of material chiefly drawn from ancient sources . . . which may be useful for further variation of the same kind'.[3] The justification for this material was the need for variety of 'a large number of English churchpeople' whose devotional life had 'found its centre in a daily celebration'[4], but the flexibility displayed here contrasted strangely with the rigid following of 1662 elsewhere. The material included the proper of seasons (e.g. ember days) and of (black-letter) saints, the common of saints, and services and memorial collects for various special intentions and occasions; the authorities drawn upon included convocations, primers, divines like Bishop Andrewes, contemporary bishops, and other churches of the Anglican

---

1 Cf Anne Dawtry, 'Walter Frere', and Donald Gray, 'Percy Dearmer', *ibid* pp 49-56 and pp 71-76.
2 p vii.
3 p viii.
4 p ix.

Communion. Despite its title, *The English Liturgy* was also published in editions with the American or Scottish communion offices, while its additional collects and lections were included in an enlarged edition of *The Sanctuary*, a communicant's manual edited by Percy Dearmer and published by Rivingtons in 1905; this too went into several editions and was still in print in 1950. Dearmer was also editor of *The English Hymnal*, which was first published in 1906[1] and for eighty years was the favourite hymn book in anglo-catholic churches of every shade. It was the first popular hymn book to include introits, graduals etc for Sundays and holy days; their provenance was Sarum, and henceforth choirs would be singing Sarum propers even when the priest's missal printed Roman propers.

In 1904 a Royal Commission on Ecclesiastical Discipline was appointed. In 1906 it recommended first that ten practices 'of special gravity and significance'—the chief being 'the interpolation of the prayers and ceremonies belonging to the Canon of the Mass'—'should be promptly made to cease', and secondly that

> 'Letters of Business should be issued to the Convocations with instructions . . .to frame, with a view to their enactment by Parliament, such modifications in the existing law relating to the conduct of Divine Service . . . as may tend to secure the greater elasticity which a reasonable recognition of the comprehensiveness of the Church of England and of its present needs seems to demand.'[2]

Perhaps because of the impact of the Royal Commission, but more probably because of the convictions of its compilers, the next missal—published by the Society of St Peter and St Paul—largely ignored the Gelasian canon. The SSPP[3] was founded in 1910 with the object of standardizing the ritual and ceremonial of the Roman party. It had no love for Sarum and at times could appear almost extravagantly ultramontane and even adolescent in its provoking of the episcopate; yet it was far from being uncritical of Rome, it had a deep love for the 1549 rite and it took seriously the politics of Prayer Book revision. The prime mover in the society was Maurice Child, then curate of St Andrew, Haverstock Hill, but ultimately secretary both of the Anglo-Catholic Congress and of the Church Union. Closely associated with him were two Oxford dons, Ronald Knox and N P Williams, and Samuel Gurney, a director of the Medici Society.

The publications of the SSPP were quickly noted for their elegance, and in 1912 it issued a superb volume, printed throughout in red and black by the De La More Press on sheets 14" x 9.5". Although entitled *The Music of the Mass*, the book was essentially an adaptation of the 1662 communion to the Roman mass, with the usual private prayers and ritual directions and a similar adaptation of 1549 in an appendix. There were also a number of miscellaneous items—the asperges, the nuptial mass and the mass for King Charles the Martyr (some of

---

1 A revised edition was issued in 1933. This was replaced in 1986 by *The New English Hymnal* which omitted the traditional propers.
2 G K A Bell, *Randall Davidson*, (1935), 1:470-72.
3 Cf E W Kemp, *N P Williams*, 1954, pp 31-41; E Waugh, *Ronald Knox*, 1959, pp 112-18.

which, like the 1549 rite, could be obtained separately)—and, although there was no kalendar, the rubrics clearly contemplated such 'advanced' feasts as the Sacred Heart and the Holy Rosary. The whole ethos was Roman, but there was also an eclecticism which was to prove characteristic of the society and which was ultimately to frustrate its aim of 'standardizing' the Roman use. In the communion, the commandments were replaced by the kyries and relegated to an appendix. The prayer for the church was ingeniously arranged in seven parts headed 'the secret prayers'. The exhortations were omitted altogether, while the communion devotions were again relegated to an appendix and printed with Roman additions as 'The form of Ministering Holy Communion' for use 'when Holy Communion is to be given in the Mass'. Five Roman prefaces were added, each accompanied by an appropriate 1662 offertory sentence and a 1549 communion sentence, but it was in the canon that eclecticism reached its peak. The canon began with the prayer of humble access, continued with 'commemoration of the living' and 'within the action', then took up the 1662 prayer of consecration, which was linked by 'wherefore' to the prayer of oblation within which was incorporated a 'commemoration of the dead'. The Lord's Prayer was printed immediately after the canon, and the ablutions were printed immediately after the communion. The only real concession to 1662 was the positioning of the gloria before the blessing—though this was somewhat negated by the printing of the last gospel after the blessing. But the omission of most of the Gelasian canon indicated a real desire for a distinctively Anglican use of some kind even among a group who in most respects seemed ardent Romanists, while the printing of the prayer of oblation immediately after the prayer of consecration represented not only a following of Overall's seventeenth-century usage, now advocated by W H Frere[1] and as an 'irreducible minimum' by Lord Halifax and others[2], but also a prophetic pointer to later usage.

The Music of the Mass represented only the first stage in the SSPP's progress towards a complete missal, and in the absence of this its sheets were 'printed so that they may be incorporated into existing missals'. Quite independently of SSPP, however, a complete missal did appear that same year when W Knott published the first edition of *Missale Anglicanum: The English Missal*, which, though nothing like as sumptuous, was also printed in red and black on very large sheets. Compiled by Henry William Gordon Kenrick who was vicar of Holy Trinity, Hoxton, from 1905 to 1937, *The English Missal* was very similar in its general conception to *The Ritual of the Altar*, but its contents were more comprehensive and its arrangements more consistent. Its kalendar was fuller, with Roman feasts in italics as well as Prayer Book ones, and the ordinary and canon provided a straightforward combination of everything in 1662 with everything in *Missale Romanum*. Nothing at all was omitted and—except for

1   *Some Principles of Prayer Book Reform*, 1911, pp 190-95.
2   Cf A Riley, *Prayer Book Revision: The Irreducible Minimum*, 1911, p 9.

the gloria which was provided for but not printed at the beginning—the Roman text was printed even when it involved an audible interpolation into the 1662 rite, and even when it duplicated or directly contradicted it. Indeed, although both rites were printed in the same type, the Roman was given implicit priority: its provisions always preceded the parallel provisions of the Prayer Book, and its accompanying rubrics were printed in larger type. Unlike its predecessors, therefore, *The English Missal* made no attempt to present a single coherent rite which could be used *in toto*, and it was left to the individual celebrant to make the final selection. But apart from the English kyries as an alternative to the commandments, the selection was limited in advance to material which had the explicit authority of Rome or Canterbury, and improving features from other sources were strictly excluded.

The next ten years were chaotic from a bibliographer's standpoint. *The English Missal* was the subtitle of a particular book, *Missale Anglicanum*. Eventually, it was to become firmly linked with that book and to be known as *The English Missal* even though the original Latin title was retained. But *The English Missal*, or even more *English Missal* without the article, could also at this time describe any missal in English. Indeed, in 1915 SSPP actually produced a sheet entitled *English Missal Containing the Ordinary and Canon of the Mass, set forth for use in the Provinces of Canterbury and York together with the Proper for Sundays and Holy Days and the Common of Saints, Votive Masses, and Masses of the Dead* as a title-page not for a new book of its own but for the use of those who wished to bind *The Music of the Mass* into an existing missal. An altar book of this period with *English Missal* on the spine and the SSPP motif of the agnus dei on the cover might prove on inspection to be the Sarum *Altar Book* of 1894 (or its second edition which appeared in 1914) with or without a few or all sheets of *The Music of the Mass* bound up within it. Similarly, Kenrick's book might have the simple title *Missal* on the spine, while the contents might be pure *Missale Anglicanum*, or *Missale Anglicanum* augmented again with a selection of sheets from *The Music of the Mass* or indeed all of its sheets. It was calculated now 'on good authority' that eucharistic interpolations were currently being made by between 2,000 and 3,000 of the clergy[1], and such clergy bought not a ready-bound book as they might today, but a variety of unbound sheets to arrange, combine, bind and title as they saw fit.

But there were still some anglican catholics—of the 'free catholic' kind—who were satisfied by none of the existing books, and for them H R Allenson published *The People's Missal* in 1916. This was compiled by Ernest Alfred Leslie Clarke, who was curate of the Ascension, Lavender Hill, from 1912 to 1916 and later vicar of Golant in Cornwall, and it was shaped 'under a vivid assurance that the Church is again called to renew herself in worthiest sincerities, and to arm herself with widest sympathies in every direction, religious and humane,

---

1   W J Sparrow Simpson, *op.cit*, p 145

if she is to lead the Coming Age of this world into the Kingdom of God.'[1] Its combination of optimistic liberalism, free catholicism and lofty patriotism met with an immediate response; a second, revised, edition was published by A R Mowbray in 1919, and further impressions were issued in 1922 and 1929. It had been hoped to publish an altar book at the same time as the people's edition. but this proved impossible and the altar book did not appear till 1920. *The Missal, Being the Priest's Edition of 'The People's Missal'* was a folio volume 'lettered after the manner of the tenth-century English scribes' and it described itself as 'A Catholic Altar-Book, after the Sarum Use, with Private Devotions from other ancient sources, national and universal, for English-minded folk both clerical and lay'. Very sensibly it contained only what was actually required at the altar: the ordinary of the holy sacrifice (with ritual music); the 1662 collects and lections; and in smaller type supplementary collects and lections for black-letter days and other 'memorable occasions'.

Many features of the rite in *The Missal* were familiar—the Lord's summary and kyries, the benedictus and the last gospel—but there were also many idiosyncrasies. The bidding prayer was inserted after the creed, a mass of Eastern material was intermingled with the Sarum offertory, a Mozarabic prayer followed the benedictus, and this in turn was followed by 'Private Devotions for use of Priest and People, based upon and following with some freedom the ancient Canon of the West, as in Sarum and National Uses, with additional help from Primitive Forms, and from Liturgies of the East'. 'With some freedom' was an understatement, but Clarke preferred his free adaptation of the traditional canon to that in 'the more primitive English Order of 1549'; he considered that the silent interpolation around the brief 1662 prayer broke 'the wearing monotony of one, long, spoken prayer' and he was confident that 'the larger devotional need of the future' would be met more by 'silent devotions' than by 'prolonged utterance'.[2] But despite its early popularity, *The Missal* was essentially a period-piece. It was withdrawn in 1933 and the remaining sheets were distributed through the Anglican Society; *The People's Missal* went out of print in 1941.

Meanwhile the SSPP was not content that its sheets should be forever bound into the missals produced by others. It quickly realized that its ignoring of the Gelasian canon in *The Music of the Mass* was far from universally acceptable, and it soon produced for binding in other missals a new set of five sheets in which the first part of the Gelasian canon was printed in parallel columns in Latin and English, followed by the 1662 prayer of humble access and the first part of the 1662 prayer of consecration in English only, and then the rest of the Gelasian canon again in parallel columns of Latin and English. It also produced in 1914, as another temporary measure, a *Missal* which was basically an abridgement of *The Coronation Prayer Book*, a special edition of 1662 published

1 Preface p.x.f.
2 Note. p xv.

by the Oxford University Press in 1902. The 1662 order was surrounded by its collects and lections, but after the sanctus there was a 28-page insertion, in identical style and type to the rest of the book, containing the Gelasian canon in Latin and English around the prayer of humble access and the prayer of consecration. At the end of the book there was a second insertion of 16 pages containing ten additional collects and lections.

But the Gelasian canon was never really approved by the leaders of SSPP whose preferences and politics were perfectly summarized by N P Williams in an SSPP tract issued anonymously in 1916:

> 'The goal we shall set before us will be, not a return to the Roman Mass in Latin, but the restoration of that magnificent English version of the Roman Mass which is contained in King Edward VI's First Prayer Book. We shall try, as far as we can, by unofficial action, to assimilate our present Mass to the 1549 Mass, in order that, when the time is ripe, the 1549 Mass may be naturally, easily and authoritatively restored. . . . Why therefore should we not take our courage in both hands, and frankly put the Prayer of Oblation back to its proper place, that is immediately after the Prayer of Consecration?'[1]

An even more extravagant (and wholly untenable[2])advocacy of the 1549 rite appeared in 1919. This claimed that the 1549 rite was 'the *same* Mass' as that which had been said in the Church of England since the days of Augustine and was still said in the Latin rite. All that had happened in 1549 was 'that English was substituted for Latin as the language of the texts'. Thus in 1547 the liturgy of the Church of England was 'the Roman mass, said in Latin'; in 1549, it was 'the Roman mass, said in English'. 1549 was both 'the last edition of the Roman mass' and 'the first edition of the Anglican Communion Service'. Events were clearly moving towards 'the restoration of this splendid rite'. Such a restoration 'ought to unite the catholic party throughout the whole Anglican communion', and to promote this great object the society would be producing an English Missal in which the ordinary and canon were those of 1549, albeit with the addition of the customary preparation prayers and prefaces and with the vague and sketchy rubrics of the original replaced by the exact and scientific rubrics of the modern Roman Missal.[3]

The society was now publishing a series of small booklets, the *Exeter Books*, to prepare the way for its new English Missal. It hoped to print both a Missal for the Altar and another for the Laity in suitable sizes, but containing the same matter, and the Exeter books were offered as drafts, in 'the English of the Book of Common Prayer', which could be freely criticized and altered before taking permanent shape.[4] Nos. 1-14 covered different parts of the liturgical year, and no.15 the preparation and thanksgiving. Nos 16-19 were advertised as containing

---

1   Didasculus, *Decently and In Order,* pp 4, 15.
2   Cf A H Couratin, *The Service of Holy Communion 1549-1662,* (SPCK, 1963), pp 8-12.
3   *Order and Canon of the English Mass: 1, Rite of 1549,* Exeter Books No.16, Preface.
4   'Note on the Exeter Books' in *Order and Canon of the English Mass 1: Rite of 1549,* Exeter Books: No. 16, 1919.

the ordinary and canon for (i) the rite of 1549, (ii) the Roman rite in English, (iii) the rite of 1918 and (iv) the Sarum rite; no. 20 the masses for Lent and no. 21 the general rubrics. But one of the three advertised as 17-19 was apparently not published since the masses for Lent appeared as no.19. In 1920 the SSPP also issued in similar format to the Exeter books *The Votive and Requiem Missal*; this book of 195 pages also included as well as the propers the ordinary and canon of 1549 (exactly as in Exeter book no. 16) and the Gelasian canon in English.

In 1921 the SSPP proudly published *The Anglican Missal* which it described as 'the outcome of ten years' work'. The title[1], it explained, was descriptive of the aim,

'To provide the whole Anglican body (and not only members of the Church of England) with a book in which it can find and follow, with devotion and intelligence, all that the priest is saying and doing at the altar in offering the Holy Sacrifice of the Mass every day of the year.'[2]

The Anglican Missal was thus, as promised in the Exeter books, as much for the laity as the clergy, and the altar-book differed from the people's only in its more varied provisions for the ordinary and canon and in the size of its margins. There were obvious advantages in linking the two so closely, but appearance was sacrificed and visually the altar edition of *The Anglican Missal* was vastly inferior to *The Music of the Mass*. It was printed throughout in black and, apart again from the ordinary and canon which were cramped, it was virtually a reprint of the 6" x 4" *Exeter books* on sheets 9" x 6". There was also advertised and maybe even published (as already noted, advertisement and publication were not always the same for SSPP) a special india-paper edition for missionaries, entitled with typical SSPP humour, *The Church Missionary Missal*.

Because of its origin in the *Exeter books*, *The Anglican Missal* had no consecutive page-numbering. A1-271 contained propers from Advent 1—Passiontide; B1-166 contained the Holy Week rites (including from B133-166 the Roman passion gospels which were optional) and Bi-lviii, again optional, the plainchant for Holy Week; C1-56 contained the ordinary and canon and the optional Ci-cii the plainchant for the ordinary and canon; D1-204 contained the rest of the proper of the season. E1-342 contained the proper of the saints, F1-92 the common of Saints, G1-156 votive masses etc and H1-140 other masses of the saints. In general these contents were much the same as *The English Missal*, though its translations—some the work of Ronald Knox and some drawn from *The English Hymnal*—were mostly superior. The main difference was that *The English Missal* was concerned with what was authoritative, and printed the whole of the Roman rite and the whole of the Anglican rite; *The Anglican Missal* was concerned with what its compilers thought desirable, and printed a single coherent rite drawn from both sources, though with basically Roman rubrics. The only exception

---

1   The title was not original. It had been used in 1869 by Mowbray for a lavishly illustrated edition of the BCP order, with collects.
2   SSPP advertisement in *Report of the Anglo-Catholic Congress*, 1923, p 197.

here was the canon where seven alternatives were offered according to the preference and province of the purchaser.

In the altar book, the 'Order of the Mass' (C1-8) began with the Our Father, collect for purity, ten commandments or kyries or 'outside the Provinces of Canterbury and York' the dominical summary, the gloria 'when it is to be said here', the collect of the day and (normally) for the King, epistle, gradual etc, gospel, creed, Roman offertory prayers concluding with the secret, prayer for the church in seven sections, invitation, confession, absolution and comfortable words. C9-18 contained prefaces without note (Anglican and Roman), C19 other prefaces 'proposed by convocation', C20-21 the Roman *communicantes* in Latin and English, and C22-24 variants from the Scottish, American and South African rites. C25-28 contained the 'Canon of the English Mass' (1549), C29-36 the Roman canon in English and Latin, C37-44 the canons of the Scottish, American and South African masses, and C45-50 that of 1662 preceded by the prayer of humble access and followed by the prayer of oblation and the Lord's prayer. C52-55 contained prayers at communion, the post-communion prayer of thanksgiving, the gloria, blessing and last gospel, and C56 contained the six 'permanent' collects from 1662.

In the lay editions different schemes were adopted according to the particular contents. Thus pages C1-24 could be the order and canon loosely based on that in the altar book but using only the 1662 canon in its 'enriched' form as in the altar book. Alternatively C 1-11 could be the ordinary of the Mass based on 1549, C12-24 the prefaces, C25-30 the Roman canon in English, C31-44 the canon of the (1549) Mass and C45-48 the order of ministering holy communion. In 1929 an abridged lay edition was issued under the title *The Shorter Anglican Missal*; here, there was consecutive pagination throughout, and the ordinary and canon—printed strangely at the back—were the loose following of 1662.

The Anglican Missal had many merits, and it was the first comprehensive altar book to offer as a form of the canon the 1662 prayer of consecration followed immediately by the prayer of oblation. But the SSPP was too controversial for its works to gain universal catholic support. In 1923 a second edition of *The English Missal* was published, and henceforth 'western' celebrants and congregations were involved in all the confusion of their different translations. There was some cooperation, however, for by arrangement with the SSPP this second edition incorporated a few phrases from the *Exeter books* in a retranslation of many prayers from Advent to Easter. It also included the Latin text of the Gelasian canon, which was printed parallel to the English text.

3.
1928-1958

The next missals were editions of the 'semi-official' revised prayer book of 1928. The story of the book's compilation and its ultimate fate are too well known to warrant repetition here.[1] In that the revision process stemmed ultimately from the unpopular 1906 recommendations of the Royal Commission, some catholics had been wary of it from the start. But none knew better than they the need for revision, and many had taken a leading part in the process. In 1914 the 'Overall' canon had been approved by the lower house of Canterbury Convocation as a permissive alternative to that of 1662, and in 1915 it had been recommended by a joint committee of both houses. At this point it had been rejected by the upper house, and when in 1918 the upper house finally approved it, it was still opposed by the upper house of York. But catholics had been encouraged by Canterbury's acceptance of it. The Exeter books had reprinted, or at least advertised, 'The Rite of 1918' and *The Anglican Missal* had included the current draft of some of the proposed new prefaces. In 1922 the new Church Assembly's revision committee issued a report in which Overall's canon was improved by the addition of an anamnesis.[2] Had this canon been accepted—or the 1549 one which was still preferred by Lord Halifax and Archbishop Lang[3]— catholics would have been more enthusiastic. As it was, there were long discussions about the position and phraseology of an epiclesis and eventually the bishops decided to insert an epiclesis in an eastern position which seemed to many people (despite the precedents of the Scottish and American rites) to break with the whole western tradition of consecration. Nonetheless the rite contained such welcome features of the unofficial missals as optional kyries, occasional salutations, additional prefaces and an optional benedictus, while the appendix contained a brief form of the preparation which was entitled 'a devotion' and propers for the lesser feasts and fasts.

In 1927, when the proposals were first submitted to parliament, some like W H Frere, B J Kidd, T A Lacey and the leaders of the Anglo-Catholic Congress movement supported them, others like the English Church Union were neutral, while a third group led by Darwell Stone and the Federation of Catholic Priests opposed them. After the Commons' rejection, however, the bishops introduced some changes into the book 'to remove misapprehensions and to make clearer and more explicit its intentions and limitations'. These changes were all in a protestant direction and, as a result of the reinsertion of the black rubric and the

---

1 Cf esp G K A Bell, *op. cit*, 2:799-802, 1325-60; W K L Clarke, *The Prayer Book of 1928 Reconsidered*, 1943; R C D Jasper, *Walter Howard Frere*, 1954, pt.1 *passim*.
2 Cf *Second Report of the Prayer-Book Revision Committee* (NA 60), sec.65, pp 62f; *Revised Prayer Book (Permissive Use) Measure* (NA 84), pp 66f.
3 Cf W J Sparrow Simpson, *op. cit* p155f; G K A Bell, *op. cit* 2:800f; J G Lockhart, *Cosmo Gordon Lang*, 1949, p 299.

new rubrics on reservation and fasting, Frere and Kidd withdrew their support and the ECU abandoned its neutrality for downright opposition.[1] But even though the book was rejected by the Commons a second time, a strict return to 1662 was now impossible, and in July 1929 the upper houses of both Convocations resolved that 'During the present emergency and until further order be taken the Bishops . . . cannot regard as inconsistent with loyalty to principles of the Church of England the use of such additions or deviations as fall within the limits of these proposals'. They gave a further boost to the rejected book by adding, 'They must regard as inconsistent with Church Order the use of any other deviations from or additions to the Forms and Orders contained in the Book of 1662'[2].

The 1928 book was duly published by the privileged presses but with a prefatory note emphasizing that its publication 'does not directly or indirectly imply that it can be regarded as authorized for use in churches'. An altar edition with the same note was published first in pica-octavo and then in English quarto. Its odd contents were based on the traditional pattern of 1662 altar books: calendar (quarto edition only); general rubrics; occasional prayers and thanksgivings; collects, epistles and gospels throughout the year; Holy Communion, 1662; a devotion before Holy Communion; Holy Communion, 1928; collects, epistles and gospels of the lesser feasts and fasts, and at a burial; litany; confirmation, 1662 and 1928; matrimony 1662 and 1928; churching of women; ordinal; accession service. The quarto edition was also issued with a special supplement, *The Music for the Celebrant*, in red and black and with the two communion services reset in larger type and specially arranged to secure a minimum of page-turning.

All the 1928 altar books were widely used, and a report issued thirty years later stated that 'the majority of the clergy abide by it [the 1929 policy] and accept the 1928 Book as having a moral, if not a constitutional, authority which they do not accord to privately printed missals'. It noted that several features of the 1928 rite—notably the Lord's summary, the kyries, additional proper prefaces, and propers for black-letter days—had achieved widespread popularity, but that the alternative canon was very seldom used and that the stricter anglo-catholics had maintained their earlier opposition to the book and had consequently rejected the episcopal policy.[3] Some of these latter argued that in 1928 the lower houses of Convocation were given no opportunity to petition the upper houses for amendments, and that this unconstitutional deprivation of their rights rendered the whole action invalid; that while the book received the approval of Convocation it did not receive its synodical concurrence; that a synod governed by the 1906 letters of business was not 'free'; and that the bishop's *jus liturgicum* was a myth.[4] For them, 'The situation,

1   For catholic opposition, cf F L Cross, *Darwell Stone*, 1943, p 163-202, and A Hughes, *The Rivers of the Flood*, 1961, pp 76-90.
2   Cf G K A Bell, *op. cit* 2:1359, and for allegations of vagueness in phraseology K E Kirk, *Beauty and Bands*, 1955, pp 60, 86f.
3   *Prayer Book Revision in the Church of England*, 1958, p 14f.
4   B J Kidd in *Report of the Second Anglo-Catholic Priests' Convention*, 1932, p 133; A Baverstock and D Hole, *The Truth about the Prayer Book*, 1935, p 69.

after the publication of the 1928 Book and the 1929 resolution remained much as it was before. Two new documents had been added to the library of English liturgical literature, but that was all.'[1]

Some clergy decided to adopt their own solutions, and shortly after the parliamentary rejection of the 1928 book, twenty-five copies (plus one on hand-made paper) were issued of *An English Missal printed for St Margaret's Church, Oxford*, a handsome volume printed by the Oxford University Press. This was compiled by Edward Wilfred Pullan, who was vicar of the parish from 1906 to 1943, and Robert Francois Marie Meade who was curate from 1926 to 1943 and later vicar of St Andrew, Worthing. The contents included the proper of the season; the ordinary and canon in red and black, with the usual private prayers and the 1662 prayer of consecration followed by the 1662 prayer of oblation; the music of the prefaces; prayers said after the prayers of the day; the proper and common of saints; votive masses; masses for the dead and sequences. In general the book laid great stress on Anglican authority: additional lections were 'selected from those sanctioned by the Bishops of Oxford since 1882, and by Convocation', and additional feasts in the Kalendar were 'taken from the Oxford Diocesan Service Book and Oxford University Kalendar'.

Respect for authority was also evident in a third edition issued in 1930 of the 1894 Sarum *Altar Book* which was 'revised and corrected in strict agreement with the rite and calendar of 1662'. The kalendar was shorn of its extraneous feasts, and their propers relegated to the appendix; the 'Order and canon of the Mass' became the 'Order of Holy Communion'; everything inserted for public recitation was omitted, and the Gelasian canon was deprived of its ritual directions and headed simply 'Private Devotions'. The Lord's Prayer however was still printed in both Sarum and 1662 positions, and two small changes away from 1662 were the placing of the ablutions immediately after the communion, and the relegation of the exhortations and invitation to the end of the rite 'for reference', so that the main text proceeded awkwardly from the prayer for the church militant to the confession.

Meanwhile 'western' catholics were active on two fronts. First, they were seeking to agree an 'interim rite' which would be a unifying factor among them and which the church as a whole might ultimately sanction. With the 1928 canon rejected almost universally, the most widely discussed schemes were those put forward in 1931 by Arthur Chandler, rector of Bentley in Hampshire but previously Bishop of Bloemfontein. His first scheme involved little more than Overall's canon, but his second scheme, produced three months later, involved a reconstruction of the whole rite along the lines of 1549, and in 1932 he abandoned both schemes in favour of 1549 *in toto*.[2] But, as the SSPP was discovering, 1549 as such was impracticable, and the use of Overall's canon, now known as that of the 'interim rite', became increasingly common—to the

1 K E Kirk, *op. cit.* p 60.
2 Cf F L Cross, *op. cit.* pp 217f. and A Chandler in *Report of the Second Anglo-Catholic Priests' Convention*, 1932, pp 128-33.

sorrow of the papalists who were saddened as they saw the Gelasian canon, their 'inalienable heritage', being exchanged for 'a mess of potage'.[1]

But despite these divisions the western catholics were also hoping to produce a universally acceptable missal. The first two editions of *The English Missal* had been Fr Kenrick's personal venture, with Knott acting as printer and selling copies on commission. But Fr Kenrick was now ageing and, after approaches to him from the SSPP, the Church Literature Association gave notice in 1932 of 'a move towards uniformity which will have sympathy from all priests'—the preparation of an altar missal which 'is to contain all the best features of the *Anglican* and *English* Missals, and will take the place of these volumes.'[2] A joint committee—consisting of F E P Langton, vicar of Holy Redeemer, Clerkenwell, and C H Scott, vicar of St Michael, Folkestone, for the SSPP with Kenrick and H L Drew, curate of St Augustine, Queen's Gate, representing *The English Missal* party—was set up to produce the new missal. But the committee soon ran into difficulties. *The English Missal* stood for literal translations; *The Anglican Missal* stood for literary ones. *The English Missal* stood for the complete Roman kalendar; *The Anglican Missal* preferred an eclectic one, with a supplement of less-favoured feasts at the end. *The English Missal* desired a supplement for Sundays after Pentecost and other Roman propers which differed from their Anglican counterparts; *The Anglican Missal* was quite content with Sundays after Trinity. It had been decided to retain the title *The English Missal* (the property of Kenrick) for the joint book, and the Church Literature Association got as far as issuing a prospectus for it in 1933, but the romanizing trend of the proposed book immediately drew the wrath of N P Williams.[3] The SSPP, disliking its translations as well as its Romanism, now withdrew its co-sponsorship and Fr Kenrick duly offered the title to Knott who in 1934 published what was simply the third edition of *The* [original] *English Missal*. In this new edition, the translations, probably as a result of the initial cooperation with SSPP, were often an improvement on those in the earlier editions. As for the contents, the Latin text of the offertory prayers was printed parallel to the English text, while the canon consisted of the Gelasian canon in English surrounding the 1662 prayer. The Gelasian canon in Latin was printed as an appendix, while the canon of the interim rite (without an anamnesis) now made its first appearance in *The English Missal* as an optional extra. There was also a supplement containing Sundays after Pentecost and other Roman propers which differed from their Anglican counterparts.

The English Missal, unlike *The Anglican Missal*, had traditionally been a volume purely for priests. But in 1933 Knott also published the first edition of *The English Missal for the Laity*, and unfortunately there was an element of confusion here. This lay edition was the personal venture of Fr Drew, who was soon to become rector of Throwleigh in Devon, with Knott again acting as printer and selling copies on commission. Drew's translations were similar to those of the 1934 altar edition, but sometimes he deviated from these so that, although both

1   A Hughes, *op.cit.*, p 39.
2   Advert in *Report of the Second Anglo-Catholic Priests' Convention*, 1932.
3   Letter in the *Church Times*, 25 August 1933

editions were clearly of the same 'family', what the layman read in the pew was not always the same as what the priest was saying at the altar. As *The English Missal for the Laity* went into further editions, the ownership remained with Fr Drew and its translations continued to differ at some points from those in the altar book.

1933 also marked the centenary of the Oxford movement, and appropriately Knott also published that year *The Oxford (Centenary) Supplementary Missal*. This was apparently the work of 'the Reverend Clement Humilis' of St Clement Cambridge, but no such clergyman appears in *Crockford's* and Clement Humilis was the *nom-de-plume* of James Tait Plowden-Wardlaw, who was vicar of St Clement's from 1931 to 1941.[1] The missal consisted of a simple version of the 1549 rite 'in anticipation of its eventual authorization' along with 'The Proper of Masses in Commemoration of Thirty-nine Beati of the Anglican Communion'. In each case the proper (which included introit, gradual, offertory, secret, communion sentence and postcommunion as well as collect and readings) was preceded by a short outline biography. The 39 were mostly heroes of the Oxford Movement, though they also included four names from the seventeenth century and one from the eighteenth, and in saluting them as 'beati' Humilis claimed 'the indirect authority of widespread appreciation of their devout and saintly lives, a national valuation which is a veritable *Vox Ecclesiae*'. He earnestly hoped that, while no priest would use the supplement at the altar 'against the expressed wish of his Bishop', there might be many dioceses where its use might be implicitly permitted.

In 1934 N P Williams, having strongly attacked the proposed new *English Missal*, conceived the idea of an *English Sacramentary* which would encourage anglo-catholics to a closer following of the Prayer Book and would be officially commended by the Archbishop of Canterbury. The general arrangement would follow strictly that of the Roman missal, even to the extent of printing the litany and baptismal office under Easter Eve, but its contents—apart from offices of preparation and thanksgiving from the *Treasury of Devotion* or the *Cuddesdon Office Book*—would be drawn entirely from 1662 and 1928. As against the quasi-official book of the privileged presses, the *English Sacramentary* would integrate the two communion rites and the two sets of propers, provide fuller music, and omit confirmation, matrimony, churching of women and the ordinal except insofar as they related to the communion; an optional supplement would be issued containing introits, graduals, etc, from *The English Hymnal*. Negotiations were entered into with a publisher and the project received the approval of Archbishop Lang, but those for whom it was intended were too much attracted by the 'interim rite' and the proposal was gradually dropped.[2]

In 1936 a new missal did appear. It was entitled *The Altar Missal*, and was published by A R Mowbray for the Society of St John the Evangelist, printed in

---

1 I am grateful to the Revd Michael Silver of Letchworth for clarifying this for me.
2 Cf E W Kemp. *op.cit.* pp 59-62.

red and black, and edited by Fr Edward Craig Trenholme, SSJE, a historian and liturgist who as early as 1910 had compiled for the society *The Hours of Prayer*. In general arrangement *The Altar Missal* followed the pattern now customary. It claimed to be 'consonant alike with the Book of Common Prayer and with the Catholic past', and, as against the *English* and *Anglican* missals, 'the main but not exclusive source' was Sarum. Roman usage was followed in some cases, but so too were the 1928 book, a collection of collects authorized by Frere and recent revisions of other Anglican provinces. In content it was somewhat briefer than some of its competitors—its provisions for Holy Week and requiems were much simpler, and there were no benedictions—and, stated the preface,

'From the point of view of authorisation, its contents should present little difficulty. Such devotional enrichments as Introits and Graduals are of the nature of anthems; and sanction for additional collects and passages of Scripture, and certain special services, is not generally regarded as impossible.'

Three orders were printed for holy communion. The first consisted of 1662, with slight rubrical abbreviations and optional 1928 omissions from the commandments; there were no audible interpolations of any kind, but silent Roman prayers, including the canon, were printed 'for optional use.' The second order included common variations and additions, supplementary rubrics, and the canon of the interim rite, 'now widely used and sanctioned' and now printed with an anamnesis, albeit a silent one. The other variations and additions included provision for the preparation (which was printed in full only under the 'general rubrics' at the beginning of the book), the full proper, kyries instead of the commandments, some 1928 offertory sentences, Sarum offertory prayers, provision for the shorter 1928 invitation, extra prefaces mostly 1928 or Sarum, the Lord's Prayer at the end of the canon, and prayers thereafter from Sarum; the gloria was printed only at the end. The third order was the South African alternative rite 'without any alteration'. Roman and Sarum music was provided for the prefaces in all three rites, while the OUP music for the 1928 prefaces was available as a supplement. No people's edition of the *Altar Missal* was ever published, though SSJE did publish in 1933 and for many years thereafter a small booklet entitled *At the People's Mass* which contained a very simple 1662-type rite, with or without the interim rite canon.

The Altar Missal, being neither thoroughly Anglican nor thoroughly Roman and with its partiality for Sarum, lacked the appeal of 1928 or of *The English Missal*, and in 1939 a revised edition of *The Anglican Missal* was issued. Though still printed only in black, the type and size (10″ x 7″) were larger than in the first edition, ritual music was printed *in loco*, the altar-book now took definite precedence, and the confusing provision for other provinces disappeared. The full contents (pp vii-xxii and 1-1345) consisted of a kalendar, the asperges, the proper of the season, a table of prayers, the common and proper of saints, votive masses, various prayers, masses of the dead and the absolution over the bier. An appendix, with separate page numbering 1-190 (shown by asterisks) contained other masses of the saints and the kalendar of the universal church. The order and canon appeared in its usual place after Holy Saturday. First (pages 1*-27*) came the 'Order and Canon of the First English Mass (1549)' with many but not all of the usual additions but without the communion devotions. Second and most important (pages 31*-139*, with prefaces with and without chant occupying pages 45*-120*) came the 'Order and Canon of the Mass, *Interim Rite*'. Almost all the usual additions were made here, but the prayer for the church took the place of the secret, the communion devotions were omitted, a public anamnesis was added for the first time to the canon and the prayer of humble access was printed instead of the usual Roman prayers after the Roman prayer for unity. 'The Form for Ministering the Holy Communion to the People' (pages 141*-142*) containing the 1662 communion devotions with Roman additions was printed at the end. An alternative arrangement, not noted in the contents page, provided in different pages 128*-141* the older arrangement whereby the Gelasian canon in Latin or English was recited around the 1662 prayer of consecration; subsequent pages were renumbered so that the rite now finished on page 154*, with the administration of communion on pages 155*-156*. The third order (p.i*-xix*), available as an option, was 1662, but still with rubrical additions and alterations, e.g. the collect of the day before the prayer for the king, and the ablutions between the Lord's Prayer and the prayer of oblation.

In 1939, the same year as the publication of the altar book, *The People's Shorter Anglican Missal* was issued, 468 pages as against 1534 (1345 + 189 for 'other masses of the saints'). The ordinary and canon on pages i -xxxiii consisted of pages 31*-44* and 123*-139* of the 'definitive' altar book, followed by the order of ministering the holy communion to the people which was identical with that on pages 141*-142* except that it also included the text of the people's general confession. But this 'people's shorter' edition was too short for some and it was followed in 1941 by *An Abridged Anglican Missal* with 690 pages. Here pages 1*-27* might consist of the 1549 'Order of the English Mass' as in the altar book, with additional collects on pages 28*-29*; these might be followed on pages i-xxxvii by the 'Order and Canon: Interim Rite' corresponding to the earlier selection in the shorter book. Alternatively, there might be the prefaces with solemn and ferial chant corresponding to pages 45*- 107* in the altar book, followed by the basically 1662 order (pages 1*-xix*) as in the altar book, the order and canon of the interim rite (pages i-xxxvii) and 'The Order of the Communion' (pages 33*-38*).

The translations of *The Anglican Missal* were also adopted in 1953 when the CLA published *A Daily Missal* for laity. But *The Anglican Missal* did not have the field to itself. None of its three orders was printed with any great respect for its normal or authorized form, and its altar edition was more cumbersome and less elegant than *The English Missal*. Its second edition was followed a year later in 1940 by a fourth edition of *The English Missal*, which was largely unaltered except that the Gelasian canon in Latin, though printed in larger type, was now an 'optional' like the canon of the interim rite. In 1943 there followed a second edition of *The English Missal for the Laity*, which was reprinted with alterations in 1949.

The next development was occasioned by the Roman Catholic revision of the holy week rites. In 1951 the 'restored paschal vigil' on the night of Holy Saturday was encouraged in place of the anticipated first Mass of Easter on the morning of Holy Saturday, and this was made mandatory in 1955, along with other changes to the rites. In 1952 Knott published an altar book, *The Order for Holy Saturday according to the English Missal together with The Alternative Order appointed to be used when the Paschal Vigil is observed in the night time*, while the CLA published *The Order for Holy Saturday when the Restored Vigil is observed*. Further changes after the publication of these books were subsequently printed on a separate sheet. In 1957 Knott published *The Holy Week Book*, and the CLA published *The Order for Holy Week*; the latter had the advantage in that it contained the text for every day in holy week as well as the full text of the ordinary and canon (Interim Rite and Gelasian) so that it did not require any other altar-book, and a second edition in red and black was published in 1965.

In 1957 a second edition of *The Altar Missal* was issued with only minor changes, but in 1958 a fifth edition of *The English Missal* appeared and here the changes were more radical. Apart from an improvement in translations, Roman collects and lections, where different from the Anglican ones, were brought forward from the supplement to the main body and printed immediately after their Anglican counterparts; the proper of Sundays after Pentecost was similarly brought forward and printed immediately after that of the corresponding Sunday after Trinity, and the proper for feasts peculiar to England and Wales and to Scotland followed the proper of saints. The Mass texts were also rearranged, though still distinguished by respect for authority. The 1662 order was printed first *verbatim* but in small type except for the prayer of consecration. Then came the Roman rite in full, but with the interpolation of the 1662 prayers for the church, of humble access, of consecration/oblation, and of thanksgiving. This was followed by the Roman order of the administration of Holy Communion, and the Roman canon in Latin. In a special edition for America, the canon of the American Prayer Book was incorporated, along with collects, lections and prefaces peculiar to that rite. Knott also issued in 1958 a second edition of *The Requiem Missal* which was produced in conformity with the new edition of *The English Missal*, and a fourth edition of *The English Missal for the Laity*.

No complete 'unofficial' altar book has been produced since 1958, and it is fitting that *The English Missal* should have been the last for it was much more widely used than its rivals, even though its contents were much more Roman than the theology or practice of some of its users. The solution to this apparent paradox is that *The English Missal*, though itself unauthorised, consistently printed everything Anglican and everything Roman, as against the private preferences and prescriptions offered by its rivals. Private judgment is bound to be exercised at some point, but *The English Missal* restricted it to material which was in some sense authoritative. The main criticism of *The English Missal* is not so much its Romanism as its studied rejection of 1928, due possibly to copyright difficulties but much more probably to the ongoing Catholic opposition to that book. But 1928 had at the very least as much claim to authority in the Church of England as the Roman rite, and *The English Missal* would have been a better book if it had included 1928 provisions and omitted, for example, the Roman alternatives to the 1662 propers.

4.

The Modern Period

A new era began in the 1960s, and there were three good reasons why full alternative altar books were no longer produced. First there was the passing in 1965 of the Prayer Book (Alternative and Other Services) Measure. This facilitated the process of liturgical revision in the Church of England and led quickly to the authorizing in 1966 of the Series One communion service—in which the Overall canon was at last made legal[1]—and in 1967 of the Series Two service. But both these services were authorized for limited periods only, and this was not conducive to the production of expensive altar books with a normal lifetime of twenty or thirty years. A lay edition of the Series One rite with collects and readings from the Revised Standard Version was published in 1967, and there was a similar edition with just the collects and readings, but the altar book contained only the rite itself. An altar book, entitled *Readings for Holy Communion* and using the New English Bible, was subsequently published by the university presses in 1970, but although this contained the collects it did not contain the rest of the rite. For Series Two, at least one priest, Fr Arnold of Cowley, immediately produced his own sheets for the thanksgiving, and these were wholly faithful to the authorized text except that they added unauthorized requiem alternatives for the agnus. The official altar book again contained the full rite along with the music of the thanksgiving, though Knott subsequently obtained permission to publish a special 20-page edition of the rite in which the authorized text was of necessity followed *verbatim*, but the arrangement and typography had a more catholic 'feel'; this edition was available either separately or bound up with the 1958 edition of *The English Missal*.

The second reason for the failure to produce complete altar books was that the Church of England was not alone in revising its rites. In 1963 the Second Vatican Council in its *Constitution on the Sacred Liturgy* gave notice that there would be major revisions in the Roman rite.[2] These began with greater encouragement of vernacular masses, for which tentative translations of the existing rite were issued. Then in 1969-70 a new *Ordo Missae* and a new lectionary were published, but it was not until 1974 that a definitive English translation of the new *Ordo* was issued and in the meantime, with the Roman situation as unclear as the Anglican, a 1969 letter to priest-members of the Church Union announced,

'With the revision of eucharistic rites existing altar books become progressively less useful; and it has therefore been decided to issue no further impressions of the *Anglican Missal*. . . . To replace it a loose-leaf missal is to be produced, incorporating material in current use, and allowing for the addition of fresh material as it appears. Its preparation is now on foot; and if all goes according to plan the work will be published in sections.'

1   Cf J M M Dalby, 'Alternative Services: The Canon of Series 1' in *Church Quarterly Review*, clxviii (1967), pp 442-51.
2   Cf W M Abbott, *The Documents of Vatican II*, (1966), pp 137-78.

But although a loose-leaf missal was produced with the temporary translations for Roman Catholic use, nothing more was heard of this proposed Anglican venture.

A third reason for the lack of complete missals was the growing similarity between the Anglican and Roman rites. The adoption of similar translations for the gloria, creed, sanctus, Lord's Prayer and agnus dei was aided by the work of the International Consultation on English Texts and, while Anglican revisions tended to adopt a more Roman structure, the Roman revision tended towards a more Anglican simplicity. There was also the Anglican canon B5 promulged in 1969 which allowed the minister discretion to make 'variations which are not of substantial importance' in any authorized service. All this led to the appearance on Anglican altars of Roman missals or sacramentaries, often with a few handwritten or pasted amendments and with an authorized canon— or something resembling it—stuck in.

As an illustration of this, in 1971 Knott and the SSPP joined together to produce *The Revised Order for Holy Week* which took into account the latest Roman changes and translations, but adopted the Series Two form of the renewal of baptismal vows in the Easter Vigil. But this book was essentially a temporary supplement to the existing ones, and in 1972 the two Anglican publishers joined with the Roman Catholic publisher Geoffrey Chapman to publish an Anglican edition of the *Holy Week* altar book which Chapman had produced for Roman use. This Anglican edition was essentially the straightforward Roman text with an Anglican addenda consisting of the references for the readings for Anglicans who might not have access to the Roman lectionary. There was also a separate sheet with references from the readings from the proposed two-year lectionary and a separate insert stuck into the text containing 'alternative renewal of baptismal promises for Anglicans (series 2)'.

In 1973 Series Three was authorized. The Series Three altar book again contained only the rite itself along with very simple music, although a version of the traditional music was produced by St Mary's Press, Wantage. For the two-year lectionary which was now authorized alongside the rite, the university presses produced another volume of *Readings for Holy Communion* from the New English Bible, but this time the collects were omitted, largely because the collects designed to accompany the new lectionary were not authorized until 1977. At the same time the Church Information Office published its own desk-size edition of *The Lessons for Holy Communion Series Three*. Here the readings were drawn variously from the New English Bible, the Jerusalem Bible and the Revised Standard Version according to the preference of the Liturgical Commission for each passage. But both books covered only Sundays and Holy Days. It was not until 1979 that a daily eucharistic lectionary was authorized, and this was derived 'with some adaptation' from the provisions of the Roman *Ordo Lectionum Missae*. English translations of the Roman lectionary were already available in both the Jerusalem Bible version and the Revised Standard version, so no separate Anglican book was issued and for the first time Anglicans could use parts of a Roman eucharistic book with explicit authority.

The separate printing of rite and readings was unusual, though not unknown, in the Church of England. It was partly influenced by the fact already noted that all the 'series' rites were authorized only for limited periods, but it was also influenced by the reforms in the Roman Catholic church whereby the missal and the lectionary were now clearly distinguished. The missal, for use at the president's chair and at the altar, became more like an ancient sacramentary and contained essentially the ordinary and canon along with the entrance antiphon, opening prayer, prayer over the gifts, communion antiphon and prayer after communion. The readings and the gradual psalm were reserved for the lectionary. Inevitably Anglican styles of celebration were affected by the Roman developments, and a distinction between the altar-book and the lectionary became increasingly acceptable among Anglicans, though the distinction was blurred in that the collects—where available—were sometimes located with the lectionary rather than with the 'presidential' rites.

Despite the obvious difficulties, the failure to issue an Anglican 'sacramentary' at this period was not due to lack of effort, for in 1973 the *Church Observer* stated that it was the intention to publish a completely new missal which would be a joint publishing venture by Collins, CLA, SSPP and Knott, and would be an off-shoot of the new Roman Missal which Collins and Goodcliff-Neale hoped to publish. It would contain a convenient arrangement of all the Anglican material for the mass, Series 1,2,3, all seasonal variations and collects (but not the readings) as well as the full text of the latest Roman Missal including the general instruction, collects, prefaces and other propers. Provided there were no hitches, the new missal could be ready by Easter 1974. But there were hitches. The next edition of the *Church Observer* announced that the new *Roman Missal in English* had been delayed until at least Low Week, and that the Anglican copyright-holders were insisting that the three series should be reproduced in their original format 'so that the ingenious arrangements that we had devised to make the Missal easier to use will have to be given up'. By the summer, the new and definitive edition of the Roman missal was still not available, while from the Anglican side it was becoming clear that Series One and Two were likely to be replaced by Series One and Two Revised, Series Three was likely to be 'very extensively revised' before it took on a definitive form, and the copyright difficulties still persisted. By winter 1974 the mood had changed, and the *Church Observer* published an article, 'The English Missal— End of a Chapter'. The new Roman Missal would now be published in January 1995, but the copyright-holders of the Anglican rites had continued to demand that the various series should be printed *verbatim* 'with all their confusion of arrangement and rubric' and had eventually withheld permission altogether. Thus 'our attempt to relaunch the *English Missal* in an up-to-date version has been shipwrecked on the shoals of Copyright'. But there was still hope of a kind,

'We have not given up our intention of publishing a new edition, and the matter will be kept continually under review; but it will certainly not be within the next few months, and it will not be in the form we had hoped for; this is not the end of the book—but it is the end of a chapter.'[1]

Series One and Two Revised, containing the eucharistic prayers of both rites, was eventually authorized in 1976 and this authorization was followed by the publication of an altar book with music. The CLA also issued a *Missal Pack for the Eucharist using traditional texts*. This consisted of a card for the first part of the Mass for use at the lectern or chair; an altar card; and the parts needed at the altar on single sided sheets for 'tipping into existing missals'

The General Synod was now busy consolidating the process of liturgical revision, and 1980 saw for a while the end of the period of experimentation, the authorization of *The Alternative Service Book 1980*,—initially for ten years but ultimately for twenty—and the gradual withdrawal of authorization from the various 'series' rites. There were two rites for holy communion: Rite A in modern language contained four eucharistic prayers and Rite B in traditional language contained two; in each case the last prayer was that of the 'interim rite' A handsome altar book was produced, and this consisted essentially of the Calendar; Holy Communion Rite A and B; Sentences, Collects and Readings; and Music for the Eucharistic Prayers. It was printed in black and (oddly) blue[2], and a double system of pagination enabled its pages to be linked with those in the full pew edition. Gradually most of its parts became available separately.

The ASB altar book has been very widely used, but not universally. Only a few traditionalist catholics have continued to use *The English Missal*, but many have been attracted to the authorized Roman Catholic translations of the new *Missale Romanum*, while the production of catholic editions of the Anglican rites has been undertaken by the Additional Curates Society. This society was formed in 1837 to supply curates in poor and populous parishes, but in the 1970s its publishing activities expanded and it assumed a more definitely anglo-catholic identity. Bibliographically it resembles the SSPP in that its publications are not always dated, but currently it has five missals in print, all ring-bound.

The first ACS book, bound in red as *Altar Missal* and printed in black throughout though with attractive graphics, was basically a version of ASB Rite A presented in a catholic style and augmented by material from the South African Prayer Book and minimally from the Roman rite. It consisted of pages 1-34 (including both 29a and 29b) followed by proper prefaces separately numbered i-x. Alongside this, however, there is now a much fuller book, still bound as *Altar Missal* but with a maroon cover and entitled inside *The Order of Mass*. It is printed in red and black and the text has been reset, but it is still enhanced by graphics, usually different from those in the earlier book. The first part on pages 1-47 is the same as the earlier book, except that four unnumbered pages have been added with tones for the Peace. A new set of pages 1-52 contains

1   Church Observer, Winter 1973 p.30; Spring 1974 p 15; Summer 1974 p 23; Winter 1974 pp 12-13.
2   Blue had been used for 'pew' editions of Series Two, Series Three and Series One and Two Revised, but the altar books had been printed throughout in black.

37

music for the prefaces, while a third set of pages 1-189 contains the Roman prefaces with music, the Roman Eucharistic Prayers 1-3, ASB Eucharistic Prayer 3 and Communion and Concluding rites drawn from both Rome and ASB. Bound as *Altar Missal Rite B*, but entitled inside *The Holy Mass Rite B*, is a shorter book containing only one set of pages 1-49. Rite B is printed here in its rite A order with the confession at the beginning of the rite, but apart from additional Roman prefaces it is a faithful catholic presentation of the rite with the customary additions. It is beautifully printed in black and red on parchment paper.

More specialized was *The Ecumenical Marian Missal* published in 1988. The rite on pages i-xxiv was basically the Roman rite with additions from Rite A, and the four canons included were the same as in the ordinary ACS RiteA book. The following pages 1-150 contained propers (including lections) for a large number of Marian feasts and observances, with a two-page appendix for St Bernadette. A revised and enlarged edition of this book was published in 1992 as *The Marian Altar Missal*. 'The Order of Mass', which now appeared in the middle, occupied pages [1-36] of which the last four were prefaces with music, while the surrounding propers were extended to cover pages 1-177. Also specialised and much briefer is an unpaginated missal for Remembrance Sunday. This again includes readings and offers a complete rite basically Roman but with additions from Rite A. The canon in the main text is Roman Eucharistic Prayer 3, with the third ASB prayer and the ASB communion and concluding rites on separately coloured paper at the end. Lastly, not exactly a missal but clearly designed for the altar, there is *The Eucharistic Prayers (Rite A) for Concelebration*, which includes all four ASB canons, preceded by general instructions and followed by the communion rite.

From a quite different background, Hodder and Stoughton published for the Church Pastoral Aid Society and Jubilate Hymns in 1986 a volume entitled *Church Family Worship*. This comprised a hymn book, an edition of ASB Rite A and a mass of other liturgical or quasi-liturgical material which, given ASB's flexibility, could often be used at the eucharist. The edition of Rite A was a faithful following of the official text, but at the back of the book (no. 785) there was a 'Family Communion Prayer'. This bore the specific disclaimer, 'Not authorised for use in Church of England services', but it was composed by an Anglican priest, Michael Perry, with assistance from Colin Buchanan, now Bishop of Woolwich, and Michael Perham, now Provost of Derby. Buchanan had been a prominent member of the Liturgical Commission, and Perham was to become an equally prominent member, and it would be naive to suppose that the printing of the prayer was not an encouragement to unofficial experimentation.

At the official level, rites for *Lent, Holy Week and Easter* were commended by the House of Bishops in 1986 and for the period from All Saints to Candlemas, entitled *The Promise of His Glory*, in 1990. There was also an unofficial supplement to these, *Enriching the Christian Year*, compiled by Michael Perham in 1993. In 1987 the ASB collects in traditional language were published for those who used Rite B. In 1993 *A Service of the Word* provided a structure designed primarily for all-age worship which authorized almost incidentally a more flexible structure for the ministry of the word at Holy Communion; this was reprinted in 1995 in *Patterns for Worship*, a 'directory' of resource material. Ministerial editions of all these were issued for use whether at altar, desk or lectern. Most recently the Church of England has authorized its own version of the Revised Common Lectionary (a revision of the Roman lectionary) for Sundays and holy days with accompanying collects and postcommunions for use from Advent 1997, and these are embodied in two official publications: *The Christian Year: Calendar, Lectionary [references only] and Collects*; and *Collects and Postcommunion Prayers for Sundays and Festivals*. A quarto lectern edition of the readings has been issued using the New Revised Standard Version, and a smaller edition for use in the pew is available both in this version and in the New International Version.

Most of the books mentioned in the preceding paragraph are part of the Church of England's preparations for the *Common Worship* which will replace ASB in 2000, though as yet neither the eucharistic rites nor the eucharistic prayers have been finally agreed. What the official altar book or books will look like and contain remains to be seen, and what unofficial books will be issued is equally speculative. At the time of writing, however, it seems likely that rites A and B will be replaced by rites 1 and 2, and that one of the six eucharistic prayers—prayer C—will be similar to the second eucharistic prayer in Rite B and the fourth eucharistic prayer in Rite A, i.e. the old 'interim rite' canon.

5.
Conclusion

Nearly 140 years have elapsed since the first publication of *The Priest to the Altar*. Our study of that book and its successors illustrates the development of eucharistic liturgy and eucharistic thinking among catholic-minded Anglicans.

First and self-evidently there was a long and consistent desire for a rite richer than that in the Prayer Book which might include not least an explicit anamnesis-oblation and also allow such catholic practices as prayers for the dead.

Secondly there was a gradual turning away from the Sarum or English use to the Roman or Western use. Prior to the publication of *The Music of the Mass* Sarum led the field. Thereafter, and particularly with the appearance of *The English Missal* and *The Anglican Missal*, western use began to prevail and, despite the SSJE Sarum-inspired *Altar Missal*, this has continued.

Thirdly there was a desire among many devotees both of ancient Sarum and modern Rome to use at first parts, and then the whole, of the Gelasian canon which was common to both. Parts were introduced in the first edition of *The Priest to the Altar*, and the whole was introduced in the first edition of *The Ritual of the Altar*. The whole was still printed in the last (1958) edition of *The English Missal* and in several subsequent ACS books, though the catholic preference seems now to be for the Roman eucharistic prayer 3 rather than for the Gelasian canon which is retained as prayer 1.

Fourthly, there was the rise and decline of a desire for the reintroduction of the 1549 rite which first appeared in the third edition of *The Priest to the Altar* and continued to feature in *The Anglican Missal* but never featured elsewhere.

Fifthly, this desire for 1549 was gradually replaced by an acceptance of the interim rite which first appeared in *The Music of the Mass* but was eventually incorporated into all three of the major missals, was formally authorized in alternative services series one, was included in ASB in both rites A and B, and is likely to be retained in the proposed *Common Worship*.

Our study concludes at a time when there is a remarkable ecumenical convergence: the structures of the present Roman rite and those of ASB are infinitely closer to each other than those of the tridentine rite and the Book of Common Prayer, the translations of Latin texts are very similar, and the new Anglican lectionary is clearly based on that of Rome. Sadly, and crucially, the canons of the two churches still differ, but taking into account the large measure of freedom allowed in ASB to use 'these or other suitable words' and the general canonical permission to make unimportant deviations, there may be little apparent difference between the use of a Roman missal, locally amended for Anglican use, and the use of the ASB altar book, legally enriched.

THE GROUP FOR RENEWAL OF WORSHIP (GROW)

This group, originally founded in 1961, has for over twenty-five years taken responsibility for the Grove Books publications on liturgy and worship. Its membership and broad aims reflect a highly reforming, pastoral and missionary interest in worship. Beginning with a youthful evangelical Anglican membership in the early 1970s, the Group has not only probed adventurously into the future of Anglican worship, but has also with growing sureness of touch taken its place in promoting weighty scholarship. Thus the list of 'Grove Liturgical Studies' on page 44 shows how, over a twelve-year period, the quarterly Studies added steadily to the material available to students of patristic, reformation and modern scholarly issues in liturgy. In 1986 the Group was approached by the Alcuin Club Committee with a view to publishing the new series of Joint Liturgical Studies, and this series is, at the time of writing, in its twelfth year of publication, sustaining the programme with three Studies each year.

Between the old Grove Liturgical Studies and the new Joint Liturgical Studies there is a large provision of both English language texts and other theological works on the patristic era. A detailed consolidated list is available from the publishers.

Since the early 1970s the Group has had Colin Buchanan as chairman and Trevor Lloyd as vice-chairman.

THE ALCUIN CLUB

The Alcuin Club exists to promote the study of Christian liturgy in general, and in particular the liturgies of the Anglican Communion. Since its foundation in 1897 it has published over 130 books and pamphlets. Members of the Club receive some publications of the current year free and others at a reduced rate.

Information concerning the annual subscription, applications for membership and lists of publications is obtainable from the Treasurer, The Revd. T. R. Barker, 11 Abbey Street, Chester CH1 2JF. (Tel. 01244 347811, Fax. 01244 347823).

The Alcuin Club has a three-year arrangement with the Liturgical Press, Collegeville, whereby the old tradition of an annual Alcuin Club major scholarly study has been restored. The first title under this arrangement was published in early 1993: Alastair McGregor, *Fire and Light: The Symbolism of Fire and Light in the Holy Week Services*. The second was Martin Dudley, *The Collect in Anglican Liturgy*; the third is Gordon Jeanes, *The Day has Come! Easter and Baptism in Zeno of Verona*; the fourth is Christopher Irvine (ed.), *They Shaped our Worship*.

The Joint Liturgical Studies were reduced to three per annum from 1992, and the Alcuin Club subscription now includes the annual publication (as above) and the three Joint Liturgical Studies. The full list of Joint Liturgical Studies is printed opposite. All titles but nos. 4 and 16 are in print.

Alcuin/GROW Joint Liturgical Studies

All cost £3.95 (US $8) in 1998—no. 4 and 16 are out of print

1. **(LS 49) Daily and Weekly Worship—from Jewish to Christian**
   by Roger Beckwith, Warden of Latimer House, Oxford
2. **(LS 50) The Canons of Hippolytus**
   edited by Paul Bradshaw, Professor of Liturgics, University of Notre Dame.
3. **(LS 51) Modern Anglican Ordination Rites** edited by Colin Buchanan, then Bishop of Aston
4. **(LS 52) Models of Liturgical Theology**
   by James Empereur, of the Jesuit School of Theology, Berkeley
5. **(LS 53) A Kingdom of Priests: Liturgical Formation of the Laity: The Brixen Essays**
   edited by Thomas Talley, Professor of Liturgics, General Theological Seminary, New York
6. **(LS 54) The Bishop in Liturgy: an Anglican Study**
   edited by Colin Buchanan, then Bishop of Aston
7. **(LS 55) Inculturation: the Eucharist in Africa** by Phillip Tovey
8. **(LS 56) Essays in Early Eastern Initiation** edited by Paul Bradshaw,
9. **(LS 57) The Liturgy of the Church in Jerusalem** by John Baldovin
10. **(LS 58) Adult Initiation** edited by Donald Withey
11. **(LS 59) 'The Missing Oblation': The Contents of the Early Antiochene Anaphora**
    by John Fenwick
12. **(LS 60) Calvin and Bullinger on the Lord's Supper** by Paul Rorem
13-14 **(LS 61) The Liturgical Portions of the Apostolic Constitutions: A Text for Students**
    edited by W. Jardine Grisbrooke (This double-size volume costs double price (i.e. £7.90))
15 **(LS 62) Liturgical Inculturation in the Anglican Communion** edited by David Holeton
16. **(LS 63) Cremation Today and Tomorrow** by Douglas Davies, University of Nottingham
17. **(LS 64) The Preaching Service—The Glory of the Methodists** by Adrian Burdon
18. **(LS 65) Irenaeus of Lyon on Baptism and Eucharist**
    edited with Introduction, Translation and Commentary by David Power, Washington D.C.
19. **(LS 66) Testamentum Domini**
    edited by Grant Sperry-White, Department of Theology, Notre Dame
20. **(LS 67) The Origins of the Roman Rite**
    edited by Gordon Jeanes, then Lecturer in Liturgy, University of Durham
21. **The Anglican Eucharist in New Zealand 1814-1989**
    by Bosco Peters, Christchurch, New Zealand
22-23 **Foundations of Christian Music: The Music of Pre-Constantinian Christianity**
    by Edward Foley, Capuchin Franciscan, Chicago (second double-sized volume at £7.90)
24. **Liturgical Presidency** by Paul James
25. **The Sacramentary of Sarapion of Thmuis: A Text for Students**
    edited by Ric Lennard-Barrett, West Australia
26. **Communion Outside the Eucharist** by Phillip Tovey, Banbury, Oxon
27. **Revising the Eucharist: Groundwork for the Anglican Communion** edited by David Holeton
28. **Anglican Liturgical Inculturation in Africa** edited by David Gitari, Bishop of Kirinyaga, Kenya
29-30. **On Baptismal Fonts: Ancient and Modern**
    by Anita Stauffer, Lutheran World Federation, Geneva (Double-sized volume at £7.90)
31. **The Comparative Liturgy of Anton Baumstark** by Fritz West
32. **Worship and Evangelism in Pre-Christendom** by Alan Kreider
33. **Liturgy in Early Christian Egypt** by Maxwell E. Johnson
34. **Welcoming the Baptized** by Timothy Turner
35. **Daily Prayer in the Reformed Tradition: An Initial Survey** by Diane Karay Tripp
36. **The Ritual Kiss in Early Christian Worship** by Edward Phillips
37. **'After the Primitive Christians': The Eighteenth-century Anglican Eucharist in its
    Architectural Setting** by Peter Doll
38. **Coronations Past, Present and Future** edited by Paul Bradshaw
39. **Anglican Orders and Ordinations** edited by David Holeton
40. **The Liturgy of St James as presently used** edited by Phillip Tovey
41. **Anglican Missals** by Mark Dalby (September 1998)
42. **Further Sources of the Roman Rite** edited by Gordon Jeanes (December 1998)

Grove Liturgical Studies

This series began in March 1975, and was published quarterly until 1986. Each title has 32 or 40 pages. No's 1, 3-6, 9, 10, 16, 30, 33, 36, 44 and 46 are out of print. Asterisked numbers have been reprinted. Prices in 1998. £2.75.